For the first time in 400 years Catholics and Protestants are holding open and friendly discussion on vital issues of Christian faith. CATHOLIC THEOLOGY IN DIALOGUE is a substantial contribution to this dynamic conversation. Father Weigel presents a lucid and balanced survey of seven key issues affecting Catholic-Protestant understanding:

The nature of the Church
(CATHOLIC ECCLESIOLOGY IN OUR TIME)

The authority of the Bible
(THE SCRIPTURE AND TRADITION)

The role of liturgy
(SACRAMENT AND SYMBOL)

The sources of Christian belief
(REVELATION, DOGMA, AND THEOLOGY)

The role of the Orthodox Churches
(THE EASTERN CHURCHES AND REUNION)

Political and spiritual power
(CHURCH-STATE RELATIONS)

Christian unity
(ECUMENISM AND THE ROMAN CATHOLIC CHURCH)

GUSTAVE WEIGEL

is the first Catholic ever to give a founded series of lectures at Yale Divinity School. The Taylor Lectures of 1960 comprise the first three chapters of this book. With Robert McAfee Brown, Father Weigel won the 1960 Brotherhood Award of the National Conference of Christians and Jews for their book AN AMERICAN DIALOGUE. Since 1948 Father Weigel has been professor of ecclesiology at Woodstock College in Maryland.

Catholic Theology in Dialogue

Catholic Theology in Dialogue

GUSTAVE WEIGEL, S.J.

Harper & Brothers, Publishers
New York

CATHOLIC THEOLOGY IN DIALOGUE

Printed in the United States of America

FIRST EDITION

H-L

Grateful acknowledgment is made to the following for permission to reprint in revised form material previously published:

Lancaster Theological Seminary: "Ecumenism and the Roman Catholic Church" in *Theology and Life*, Vol. 3, No. 4, November 1960.

Helicon Press, Baltimore: "Church-State Relations: A Theological Consideration," a brochure, published 1960.

Fordham University, Russian Center: "The Eastern Churches and Reunion," a pamphlet published by *One Fold*, 1960.

Library of Congress catalog card number: 61-13284

Imprimi potest: John M. Daley, S.J., *Praep. Prov. Marylandiae.*
Nihil obstat: Edward A. Cerny, S.S.
Imprimatur: ✠ Francis P. Keough, D.D., Archbishop of Baltimore, May 2, 1961.

Harper

Contents

Foreword

The present work gathers together lectures given to non-Catholic audiences on theological themes of interest to those in search of Christian unity. The first three chapters were given as the Taylor Lectures of the Fiftieth Annual Convocation of the Yale Divinity School in Easter Week of 1960. Friends at Yale were kind in their reaction to the papers. Perhaps I have succeeded to some degree in translating Catholic expressions into a language better known to non-Catholics. If this be the case, it might not be useless to offer the lectures to a wider public. It is with such a hope in mind that this book is presented.

I was told that I was the first Roman Catholic to give a founded series of lectures at Yale Divinity School. It is out of a feeling of gratitude that I wish to give witness to the great friendliness which was shown to me at Yale. Fraternal courtesy and unfeigned good will surrounded me during my happy stay in New Haven. In particular I wish to thank my friends, Dean Liston Pope and Professor Robert Calhoun, for their warm and easy hospitality.

The last four chapters contain lectures given on other occasions. Every occasion presented an opportunity of conversation with Christians not of my church. Two studies were directed to the Eastern Orthodox whose importance in the present ecumenical dialogue becomes more evident each day.

GUSTAVE WEIGEL, S.J.

Woodstock College
May, 1961

I

Catholic Ecclesiology in Our Time

It will become evident to all that certain concerns and positions in Catholic theology can also be found in its Protestant counterpart. This is not strange. At a given moment, there is a prevailing wind which affects all the people in a given area. Under the pressure of this wind, all will react to it. Different people will react differently, but all the reactions will be functions of the same force working on all.

Because ecclesiology is my own specialization, I might by prejudice think that it is the most vital branch of Catholic theology. I do think so; but I do not think that it is mere prejudice which has led me to this position. At any rate, ecclesiological meditation is conspicuous in our time and we must deal with it.

The Church has been with us since the days of the apostles. Much is said of her in the New Testament, and yet nowhere in Scripture is she defined. Nor did the councils of the Church nor yet any pope supply us with such a definition.

Many of the Fathers of the Church speak of the Church in connection with some other theme. Clement of Rome, Ignatius of Antioch, Polycarp, Irenaeus of Lyons, John Chrysostom, Leo the Great, and John of Damascus supply us with many ecclesiological insights, though they did not do so systematically nor in formal treatises. Augustine must be mentioned in particular because he has so much to tell us about the idea of the Church, in spite of the fact that he never prepared a systematic ecclesiology. There were indeed formal treatises on the Church in the early Fathers. Cyprian, Optatus, and Pacian wrote such ecclesiological tractates but they did not try to give an ecclesiological synthesis. In a word, the Fathers give us much material for ecclesiological investigation but they do not give us a formal ecclesiology.

In the early years of the Middle Ages theoretical ecclesiology received no attention. Instead, there was much canon law being written. Here is another instance where data, but only data, are given to the ecclesiologist. Even in the thirteenth century, the bloom time of the Middle Ages, the great masters who gave us the classical division of theology did not include a treatise on the Church. St. Thomas in his *Summa theologica* deals with the Church briefly in terms of the Mystical Body of Christ as an appendage to his Christology. Many ecclesiological ideas are present in his treatment of the sacraments, but there is no ecclesiological treatise as such. The same may be said for the other great Scholastics of the thirteenth century. The reasons for these oversights are not evident to us, but certainly Peter Lombard's *Book of the Sentences* in the twelfth century was used as a basic guide by all, and the Lombard does not propose a formal ecclesiology.

The fifteenth century was a period of strife between the princes and the popes. In this period Juan de Torquemada, O.P., wrote his *Summa de ecclesia*, which sounds like a sytematic ecclesiology but really was not. He was defending the primatial rights of the pope over Christendom. There was much ecclesiological writing in this century but it was primarily concerned with the place of the Bishop of Rome in the unwritten constitution of the *res publica christiana.*

Ecclesiology as a formal theological discipline was born in the sixteenth century as a direct result of the Protestant Reformation. But the tractates on the Church all suffer from one common defect. Catholics and Protestants were engaged in bitter polemics. It was the time of Controversial Theology, in many ways fruitful but essentially quarrelsome. By the time of the nineteenth century Protestantism was not too concerned with the notion of the Church, and ecclesiological work was not too prominent. In Catholic circles ecclesiology had become a fixed part of the total theological *cursus*, but it was considered as an essay in apologetics. The quarrel with the Protestants was still manifest, but new adversaries had arisen. Rationalism plagued the eighteenth century and liberal historicism haunted the nineteenth. The work of the Catholic ecclesiologists slowly came to a point which manifested itself in the ecclesiological doctrine of the First Vatican Council; but nowhere was there a consideration of the total reality of the Church. Phases of its nature and being were examined, but a total picture was not essayed.

It was after World War I that ecclesiology became more holistic and more vital. On the Catholic side the man who brought this out into the open was Professor Karl Adam of Tübingen. His *Wesen des Katholizismus* (1924), badly rendered as *The Spirit of Catholicism* in its English translation, was a point of departure for modern Catholic ecclesiology. This book was a reaction to the Protestant Friederich Heiler's analysis of Catholic theory.

Adam used the Pauline symbol of the Church as the Body of Christ as the guiding thread of his systematic outline. This was an innovation in Catholic academic ecclesiology. All through the nineteenth century the key concept was the Church as the Kingdom of God. Nor was this idea used according to its scriptural meaning but rather after the fashion of Bellarmine's thought in the sixteenth century. Kingdom in Bellarmine's treatise was employed as a sovereign society as manifested in the Kingdom of France or the Republic of Venice.

It is interesting to see the reaction of the Catholic theological brotherhood to the work of Adam. At first it was well received, but not as a theology. It was considered as an essay in homiletic piety. Adam had not used the severe logical schematization then in use in the schools. In consequence, anything not so structured was not considered theology. For the same reason Cardinal Newman's work was not taken too seriously in theological circles.

However, in the twenties Adam's work inspired many to see in it a strict theology and they used it as such. The result was opposition from the theologians because it was an unintentional criticism of their work. They resented the introduction of the concept of the Mystical Body as the matrix for the ecclesiological treatise. They considered it quite in place in the pulpit or in spiritual reading, but it should not intrude into the theological enterprise. But much work was being done along the lines suggested by Karl Adam, and the result was a war between those who used the Kingdom of God concept as central and those who replaced it with the notion of the *sōma tou Christou*. In 1943, during World War II, Pius XII published his encyclical *Mystici corporis* which was the outline of an ecclesiology based on the symbol of the Body of Christ. After that event there could be no opposition to the newer essays in ecclesiology.

Yet it would have been too hard for the older theologians to reconstruct their treatises completely. Some continued their old efforts and added a supplement on the Church as the Mystical Body. This, however, was hardly an organic vision. Outlines for the newer ecclesiology were being offered in Europe by many theologians, but even to this moment there is no set ecclesiology in Catholic circles. To use the words of Koster, a Dutch Dominican theologian, ecclesiology is in the making.

But there are certain common trends which can be

detected in the many ecclesiological essays appearing in modern journals. Little theological centers are still following the manuals which were representative of the theology of the first years of this century. But the livelier centers have dropped that approach and are working in a newer style.

Concerning this newer style one can say something. The interest now is biblical and patristic. Ecclesiology itself is not polemical. There is a general recognition that the Church is a mystery. We can profitably explain these three outlooks.

With the revival of a biblical concern on the part of the theologians, the Scriptures, especially the New Testament, were carefully scrutinized by the divines. The use of Scripture is nothing new in Catholic theology. In fact, St. Thomas equated sacred doctrine with the science of Scripture. Yet by the end of the nineteenth century many Catholic theologians were using a method which was quasi-fundamentalist, though it could never be purely fundamentalist. Texts were taken in isolation, and they were used as rigorous philological proofs for theological theses. Key words in the Bible were indeed used, but a meaning was given to them without a thorough investigation of these ideas in their biblical context. Meanings were stuck on the words in the light of postscriptural developments and concerns. I remember my own student days in ecclesiology when the Kingdom concept was dominant in the development of the ecclesiological treatise. Yet the notion of Kingdom was not explained in terms of the biblical setting. Kingdom was understood as royal sovereignty with the functions explained by Montesquieu in the eighteenth century. Under such circumstances the biblical notion was not even touched. Rather, in its place, another idea was introduced under the guise of being biblical, although it was not.

Today this tactic would be quite impossible. The Catholic scriptural scholars would not tolerate it. Moreover, the legalistic accent so strong in the earlier treatises is unpleasant to the modern ecclesiologists, and they are anxious to be ontological rather than juridical. They also want to be vital rather than schematic. Thirdly, they are searching for the supernatural factors in the constitution of the Church.

In all these concerns the current biblical scholars and the patristic investigators have been of great aid and serve as a stimulus. The return to Scripture has led to the abandonment of the proof-text. In its place there is the total scriptural burden which must be considered. Fundamentalist literalism has been transcended, but the biblical affirmation has been kept.

However, the Catholic notion of the inseparable union of Scripture and tradition functions today as much as in the days of St. Vincent of Lérins. In recent times there has been much clarification of the meaning of tradition. It would be well for non-Catholic theologians to understand this development. In Protestant theology there is also a renewed awareness of the role of tradition in the faith of the Christian, and the work of Albert Cook Outler here in America is quite indicative of this trend. However, by and large, Protestants understand by tradition the faith of the historical church in the light of historical science. This is not true in Catholic theology. For the Catholics tradition is not a mere appeal to history; it is a strictly theological conception.

As the Catholics see it, tradition is the teaching of the Church. The same Church always teaches the same doctrine through the power of the indwelling Spirit within the Church. The magisterium under that power formulates the doctrine adequately for the moment of its teaching. Such formulation is dogma, which is the normative expression of the truth of revelation. Truth does not evolve, because there is only one truth which the Church communicates and that is the total revelation of Christ. The Church grows in awareness of the revealed truth and in that sense there is an evolution, and that evolution will become externally manifest by the progress of dogmatic affirmation. The point to be stressed is that the new dogma does not deny the old one, but rather absorbs it into a fuller constellation of meaning wherein the older dogma is completely and without inner change related to the new.

This process takes place in history but it is not an historical process. It is strictly ecclesiological. The Catholic theologian goes to older dogmas convinced that he already has the truth in them because of his adhesion to the teaching Church of his own time. In principle he can see no contradiction in what is taught now and what was taught in ages past. Nor does he try to resurrect ancient positions on the hypothesis that they have been lost later.

It is here that Catholic theology can be a scandal to

non-Catholics. The Catholic does not approach teachings of the Council of Chalcedon with the uncommitted attitude of the non-Catholic. The latter meets Chalcedon with a bag of historiographic tools and no obsessive concern for what the later Church taught. He feels free to formulate Chalcedonian thought as he sees it in its historical isolation. His findings can well go counter to the doctrine of the living Church. His conclusion will be either that the living Church ought to go back to the doctrine of Chalcedon or that Chalcedon cannot be normative for the Church of our day. Neither of these two conclusions can be accepted by the Catholic theologian. He insists that the actual Church is teaching Chalcedon and that Chalcedon will always be normative for Christian doctrine. The result will be reconciliation of positions which seem to the non-Catholic dishonest subterfuges.

This scandal is needless if the non-Catholic understands the methodology of Catholic theology. This form of divinity begins with the principle that revelation can be adequately achieved only by following the teaching of the Church to which he here and now belongs. This is definitive, normative, peremptory. Here is his commitment of faith. He cannot, as a Catholic, theologize in any other way because theology is the intelligent formulation of faith. It does not create a faith; it is itself a product of a faith which is already there. If the theologian questions his faith he has already lost it. He is on the road to making a faith rather than attempting to understand the faith he has.

For the Catholic, the Protestant readiness to question any dogma with the inner freedom to reject it, seems something less than faithfulness. As the Catholic sees it, the construction of a faith is not the task of theology. Its proper function is to understand the faith which is there. The Catholic cannot quarrel with it without abandoning it. When this happens, he is not the follower of Christ but turns out to be a new prophet. Concerning his prophetic claims no judgment need here be made. Suffice it to say that he who abandons the faith once and for all delivered to the saints is not a Christian. The Catholic has made his decision to cling to that faith and no other.

The trend to reconstructionism which is highly visible in Protestant theology deeply puzzles the Catholic. The freedom presupposed in the reconstructionist enterprise is undoubtedly alluring; but the Catholic simply cannot understand how such freedom can be tolerated by the commitment of faith.

This brings up the current Catholic ecclesiologist's conception of the Church. This is a matter of greatest importance to Catholicism itself. The Catholic proposes an equation wherein the equal signs are not indications of equality but of equivalence. God, Christ, and Church: these three terms are ultimates. Usually Protestants find this doctrine to some degree scandalous and we had better explain the terms and their relations.

God is the transcendent ultimate, the ground of being, and man's ultimate goal, his *telos*. Union with God is the destiny for which man is created. This destiny is now physically impossible because of man's congenital alienation from God through what in theology is called Original Sin. Yet God, in gracious condescension, deigned to overcome for man his radical estrangement, and revealed Himself and His saving purpose progressively until the definitive revelation and salvation was achieved in the incarnation of God in Christ Jesus. This was the high moment of history, ushering in the final stage of human existence in preparation for the posthistorical eschatological era.

The historic Jesus of Nazareth was truly God and truly man. In Him the ideal of man's union with God was absolutely perfect in its achievement. It could not be verified exactly in any other man because other men had human personalities, while Christ's personality was formally divine. Yet a pattern had been set ontologically. If the concrete human nature of Christ could be shared with other men, then all things would be given to mankind. In Christ a concrete historical humanity was eternally united to divinity. Sharing, then, in Christ's humanity, any man would be bound internally and objectively with God. If man shared the human nature of Christ, he would be living in Christ. His would be the position of a co-heir of all the promises.

The Incarnation must therefore be considered not merely as one historical event but as a total re-creation of the human situation. This re-creation was simultaneously the creation of the Church. There are some forty symbols used for the Church in the New Testament. All give us insight into her being and none must be overlooked.

But of them all, the richest and most revealing is Paul's daring symbol of the Church as the Body of Christ.

In this symbol the Church is an organism as much as an organization. There is one life, and that is the life of Christ transfused in all the members by the Spirit of Christ, the Holy Ghost. The Church is thus more than a means of salvation; it is salvation already achieved as far as the present human condition allows. When the Christian shares death with Christ his salvation through resurrection will be complete.

The Church is, then, Christ prolonged in history until He comes again in judgment and power. Christ is here and now in the Church. Moreover, we must avoid the notion that this is purely figurative language. Figures of speech are only external analogies, but the analogy of the Church with the living body of Christ is intrinsic and ontological. It is, of course, an analogy beyond a doubt; but an analogy which discloses reality as it truly is. In Catholic circles the *sōma tou Christou* is usually translated as the Mystical Body of Christ. The word *mystical* fulfills three functions: (1) it distinguishes the present earthly body of Christ from the body that walked the roads and streets of Palestine; (2) it distinguishes the Church from the Eucharistic presence of Christ; (3) it indicates that the Church is the body of Christ by analogy rather than material reality.

Now the point to be stressed is that intrinsic analogy objectively describes reality in terms of proportional equivalence. It does not ascribe a term in univocal identity. There is here no instance of literalism, but on the other hand there is more than a transfer of language.

The consequences of this understanding of the Church as the Body of Christ are many. All of the Christ-functions are performed by the Church in analogous language with Him. He was the revealing prophet, king, priest, redeemer, sanctifier, judge, and healer. Within the limits of analogy the Church must have the same attributes. The definitive revelation came from Christ, and so it must now come from the Church. Sanctification came from Christ and Him alone, and so it must now come from His Mystical Body. The way of true life and conduct was shown by Christ, and so now it must come from the Church as Christ continued. The heavy emphasis which Catholics place on the Church is logically inevitable in the light of the symbol of the Church as Christ's living body.

The second feature which is corollary to this ecclesiology is that the action of the Church is as symbolic as its being. The Church symbolically is Christ and her actions will be symbolic by the same reason. The sacraments are therefore the most proper action of the Church. In symbol she, the great symbol, manifests herself and does her work.

The third feature which derives from the conception of the Church as the symbolic presence of Christ is an apologetic one. The Church is made up of sinners, and yet the Christ is no sinner. The Church as an historical entity shows all the limitations of finite, defective humanity, and yet the Christ is above such shortcomings. But all the miseries of the Church are only facets of her physical being. The judge's robes may be tattered and soiled; they may fit the judge badly indeed; they may show signs of anachronism; but all these things belong to the robe as cloth. In their symbolic value and action the robes are as powerful as if they were beautifully made, beautifully fitted, and beautifully appropriate. The Church as a sheerly empirical entity will be no different from any other empirical reality. However, this is only the lesser part of her being. We must move from her historical appearance to her symbolic meaning. This ascent is, needless to say, an ascent of faith. From that vantage point what is seen is the Christ, that same Christ who in His own journey to death was a scandal to the faithful of his time: poor, tired, depressed, and persecuted. To see in Him the incarnation of God, the anointed of the Most High, required a revelation from the Father, and only in such revelation could He be seen for what He truly was.

The vision of the Church as seen in modern Catholic ecclesiology is a very moving thing. It humbles and exalts the believer; it consoles and stimulates him; it puts his feet on earth and his head in heaven.

For a Christian of the Reform tradition this vision will have difficulties.

First of all, he will think of many passages in Protestant theology and worship which are echoes of the Catholic paean. But in the Protestant expressions it is the invisible Church which is praised. For the visible Church the Reform tradition has many harsh words. For the Church invisible the Protestant has as high a regard as the Catholic. He just cannot see how this admiration can be caused by the Church before our eyes. It is here that the symbol of the Mystical Body is so helpful. Although the distinction between the visible and invisible Church can be understood in a good sense, yet it is a poor distinction to follow radically. There are not two Churches but only one. That the Church has two facets which are distinct is true; but the facets, though distinct, are not separated. If the Church of Christ is the body of Christ, then she is by essence visible. Nothing could be less invisible than a body. That in this body an invisible activity is going on can be admitted without losing the value of the body symbol. Man is like that. We see his bodily actions but we do not thereby perceive his true life, which is a life of thought, insight, choice, and deliberation. There is, therefore, within the Church which is most visible an invisible vitality that somehow manifests itself even in that which is visible.

Perhaps the Christian of the Reform tradition is afraid of deriving too much from the body symbol. He may see in such derivation an affirmation of hierarchy in the Church. This he feels is too much. Yet this difficulty is nonexistent for the Catholic who does believe that the Church is hierarchically structured. For him, therefore, the body symbol is most comforting. If the Church is a body, then it is not like an undifferentiated blob of protoplasm. It will be an organism made up of different organs, differentiated from each other by structure and function. The very nature of a body demands a hierarchy of parts in order to insure unity and vital efficacy. One is the life but many are the members; nor is the eye the ear, nor the hand the foot. It spells out unity of life identical with multiplicity of distinct functions for which there are distinctly structured parts.

We all know that symbols must not be taken as allegories where every element in the proposed image has univocal verification in the reality of the thing allegorized. Symbols are greater than allegories, and they reveal great lines of reality without seeking a one-to-one relationship between the factors of the symbol and the thing symbolized. Yet the notion of a hierarchically structured, visible Church fits uncommonly well with the symbol of the body of Christ. The detailed structure of the hierarchical parts is not given by the symbol itself. Such information must be sought for elsewhere.

In spite of all that can be said for the Catholic approach to the symbol of mystical body as a deep description of the Church, I think that Protestants will be uneasy with the Catholic effort. Paul Tillich seems to go to the root of the matter. He believes Catholics put the historical Church in the place of God, and for him this is heteronomy or, in a more usual term, idolatry. From what has been said so far, we can see the grounds of Tillich's fear. On this question it seems to me that Tillich is speaking for all Protestants, although his total theology may not be acceptable to all who follow the Reform pattern of faith.

That the modern Catholic conception puts the Church

in place of God is partially true and partially false. If we understand heteronomy in Tillich's terms as the substitution of something finite and historical in the place of the transcendental God, then Catholic ecclesiologists are not heteronomists. They loudly confess that the Church is a finite and historical reality and as such cannot be God. On the other hand they make much of the doctrine of the Incarnation. This for them is the great act of Christian faith. In this faith God did identify Himself with something historical and finite: the human Christ. If this is not accepted, then Incarnation is not taken seriously. On the rock of Incarnation all theologies must be tested. Gnosticism, Arianism, and Nestorianism denied the Incarnation in one form or other, and the Church could not in loyalty tolerate their rejections.

That God is nothing finite and imperfect is a good Christian theological position. What is more, it is necessary for any Christian belief. But this does not deny that God can take into His own mysterious and infinite being something historical and finite. If it were to deny that, then the Incarnation is denied. If this is denied, then we are sinners indeed and in penance we must return to Israel according to the flesh. Israel refused the doctrine of the Incarnation as a contradiction of the infinity and perfectness of God. On this refusal it continues to exist.

Granted the transcendence of God, we must yet admit that the divine *Shekinah*, a material presence of God, is possible. The ancient rabbis saw that, even though they refused to see the *doxa* of God in Jesus the Christ, *She-*

kinah, *doxa*, the glory, are all words which tell us that God in love transcends even His transcendence. The human figure of Jesus of Nazareth was the divine *Shekinah* just as was the cloud on Sinai. The Christ *Shekinah* was prolonged and extended in time and space in the form of the Church. The cloud on Sinai foreshadowed the Christ to come, and the Church prolongs the historical Christ until the end of time.

Is God His *Shekinah?* One must answer both yes and no. It is God's real presence in time and space. It is not God's pure essence, but it is God coming to material man in love and condescension. In the *Shekinah* God is there, and only where He is, can He be met. Only in the encounter with Him in His *Shekinah* can man be saved. We have here another formula for the great ecclesiological axiom: *Extra ecclesiam nulla salus.* (Outside the Church there is no salvation.)

We have here the strong realism of Catholic theology. This is its peculiar characteristic. Its approach to revelation is ontological, not with an ontology of gnostic mysticism but with the ontology of intelligence enlightened by faith.

A Protestant may well say that this is evident enough, but is it biblical? That question is an ambiguous one. What is the meaning of the Bible in the question? Does it mean a book, self-sufficient and self-standing, which can be understood by the exclusive use of the scientific method of philology? If that is the meaning, then the answer can only be that current Catholic ecclesiology can be constructed out of the biblical data, but it is not the only construction possible. If by biblical we mean the burden of the Bible as it shows up interpreted in the unbroken preaching of the Church, then it alone is biblical. This second answer, which is the Catholic answer, supposes that the Bible and the Church are inseparably joined. The Bible is the Church's book. It is not over her or separated from her being. It can only be read profitably when read from her holding hands. To grab the book from her hands and study it in isolation is to lose the Bible. In such a human action it transforms itself from a word of God into a word of man. It no longer is salvific.

It is at this point that Catholic and Protestant ecclesiologies will divide. The Catholic's stand is simply that the Bible is in the Church and the Church is in the Bible. It is hard to formulate the Protestant stand. Certainly not all Protestants would say that the philological method is the exclusive way to understand the Scriptures. Some do say it. Yet all give the theologian and the believer a right to judge the Church in the light of their grasp of the biblical message, whether that be achieved in the light of philology, in the warmth of piety, or in the light of existence.

Here begin the divisions. The Catholic simply rejects the thought that a believing Christian can judge the Church, and by the Church he means the one Church, both visible and invisible. The Catholic, with the Protestant, believes that the prophetic protest of the Spirit must be addressed to the members of the Church so that they live up to the great ecclesiastical calling. Such protest is not against the Church but against the sinners in the Church. As the believer protests against the sinner, he must remember that he himself is under judgment; and the Church, the Christ *Shekinah* in the world, the locus of God in history, will do the judging.

The Catholic paradoxically believes that the Church, being Christ continued, is all-holy and yet made up of sinners who must be built up to the stature of the full Christ. For him the faithful are the saints, not because of their own sinlessness, but because they live, act, think, and pray in Christ who certainly is sinless because He is truly the Son of God.

II

The Scriptures and Theology

For almost three thousand years men have been studying the Scriptures. Every kind of method has been used to get real or supposed secrets out of it. The methods come and go but generation after generation, the Book remains substantially the same.

It is certainly true that for the Jewish and Christian theologian the Book is of paramount importance. Whether one believes in *sola scriptura* or in Scripture and tradition, the Book is the source of data for the theologian. St. Thomas Aquinas identified theology with the study of the Bible. Polemics between Catholics and the Reformation theologians made the descendants of Aquinas obscure his principle, but the polemics did not make the theologians abandon Scripture. If anything, they returned to the Scriptures more fervently, but their return was not pure in its motives. The Scriptures were considered to be an armory from which one borrowed weapons against the enemy. Today we think that the theologians of the sixteenth and seventeenth centuries, Protestant and Catholic, used a very defective method in their exegesis. Protestants of the eighteenth and nineteenth centuries also believed that, and they went about the exegetical task in a new way. Their way was called the critical, and later, the historical approach to the sacred page. But there was little that was sacred in it when they finished their work.

The nineteenth century was very important in the whole field of exegesis. In that century historiography was given precise rules. The work of Leopold von Ranke and Theodor Mommsen sharpened the arms of historical work, and they drew up canons for its operation. Protestant exegetes took these new orientations gladly and with enthusiasm; the Catholics were loath to do so.

By the third decade of this century it became clear to all that the unmodified and exclusive use of the tools of historicism in the exegesis of the Bible would only give us the historical dimension of the biblical burden. We might well know the complexities of the external politics of the Kings of Judah without ever knowing whether God had anything at all to do with the matter. In fact, the historicists kept God out of the Bible as far as they could.

Everyone knows that Albert Schweitzer in the first decade of the twentieth century had already exposed the fatal weakness of the historicist method of scriptural study. However, it required another decade for the voice of Karl Barth to set up a real revolt against biblical historicism. From that time on the exegetes have been far more sober in their work. The rules of historiographic research are still retained, but in the more humble spirit of the historical scientist of our age. We can call the method of heuristic argument and exegesis of our day the scientific method, but it is not the science of the nineteenth century which we are following.

Today both Catholics and Protestants are following the same methodological procedures in their analysis of the Bible. However, this meeting of minds meant that both groups had to travel in different directions in order to come to their present positions. The Protestants moved from a leftist extreme, the Catholics from a rightist extreme, until they are now close to each other in the middle.

There is no call for me to describe the hegira of the Protestant exegetes. Let me more profitably point to that of the Catholics. In the late nineteenth century the Catholic scholars examined the Scriptures with the postulate which is a matter of Catholic dogma, namely that the Scriptures were written by God in a mysterious but true fashion called inspiration. From this postulate they derived a second principle, namely that the whole book was inerrant. So far their reasoning was sound enough. Even a second corollary was not unreasonable, namely that every biblical affirmation, implicit or explicit, enjoyed the privilege of a divine oracle.

The real weakness of their efforts was due to an unvoiced assumption that every statement was or implied a logical affirmation which could be achieved by common sense. Although they had to admit, because of Catholic tradition, that there was more than one sense in Scripture, they made much of the Thomistic doctrine that all senses were rooted in the literary sense of the words. The mystical or allegorical senses were not the meanings of the words, but of the events which the words described. Hence they stayed close to the literary sense, but always on the supposition that it was, at least reductively, an instance of logical predication which could be understood adequately by common sense relying on fundamental Aristotelean logic.

This method was a long cry from the historicist methodology in use among Protestants. Its strong inclination was to criticize out much of the text and reconstruct the remainder into a merely historical account of past events. It is no wonder that Catholic exegesis had nothing to offer Protestant scholars and what the Protestants brought forth usually only served Catholics with affirmations which had to be refuted.

There are three stages in the change of Catholic biblical scholarship from its nineteenth century past to its present stand. The first stage was the last decade of the nineteenth century as it was influenced by two men: Marie-Joseph Lagrange, O.P., and Leo XIII. Father Lagrange was a great man, the founder of the French *École Biblique* in Jerusalem which has recently been so prominent in the investigation of the Dead Sea Scrolls. He also founded the valuable *Revue Biblique* which from the end of the nineteenth century to our own day has been so consistently good.

Lagrange realized that the historical method was necessary for sound scriptural investigation. He felt that the irresponsibilities of some of the men who were using it were not necessary features of it. In consequence he began to use it and reflect on its genuine structure, but there were many Catholics who were frightened by what he was doing, and they stirred opposition to the man and his work.

However, the spirit of Leo XIII, who was the pope of the time, defended the scholar. Leo himself was anxious for a Catholic biblical revival, and his encyclical *Providentissimus Deus* (1893) urged all Catholic theologians to return to the Scriptures with all the fervor manifested by the Fathers of the Church and the medieval masters. As for the historical method of exegesis, he was suspicious; but he recognized and said that it could be used, provided the inspiration of Scripture and the inerrancy of the divine oracles were not denied or put into jeopardy.

The example of Lagrange and the encouragement of Leo enticed a few theologians and exegetes to move out of the older way. They were neither many nor were they dominant.

The second stage of the evolution of present-day Catholic scriptural study corresponds to the years of the Modernist movement and its immediate aftermath. In terms of years perhaps we should consider the period from 1905 to 1925. The Catholic Modernists, whose foremost scriptural scholar was Alfred Loisy, made of exegesis an exclusively historical enterprise inspired by a strong spirit of iconoclasm. They so expounded the Bible that the basic dogmas of Catholicism were denied. Jesus was not divine; He did not arise from the dead; Paul's version of Christianity was original and illegitimate; the Church was a later crystallization of an early movement of mystical and moral enthusiasm.

Within Catholicism such doctrine is impossible. Although the Modernists indeed wanted to remain in the Church, they were indigestible. The dilemma was clear: either the Church was hopelessly in error or the Modernists were. There could be no reconciliation between the two. One of the consequences of this conflict within the Church was the rise of a theological and clerical group called Integrists. They were extremely conservative and abominated anything which even remotely resembled the Modernist thinkers. They were not only conservatives but self-appointed vigilantes. They snooped into every academic corner and hounded any scholar who did not show the spirit of ultraconservatism which was their own frame of mind. It was a period of theological McCarthyism within the Church.

Fortunately they had attacked Giacomo della Chiesa before he became Pope Benedict XV in 1914. In his first encyclical he condemned the Integrists as vicious intriguers, and with that condemnation their power was broken. Now a return to the spirit of Father Lagrange was possible, and it was soon to be fomented by Karl Barth's cry for a return to Scripture as revelation.

Although Benedict did help the progress of Catholic scriptural studies, yet he did not give men of the movement an all-clear signal. In his own encyclical on biblical studies, *Spiritus Paraclitus* (1920), he showed himself reluctant to accept some of the theories of the newer men and was rather negative in his appreciation for the work done. He did not condemn the new men or their methods, yet it was clear that they had to move with something less than full speed ahead.

As a consequence, the movement marched on slowly. Looking back Catholics feel that this was just what was needed. There was still sporadic opposition, but it was weak; and even this finally was given the *coup de grâce* by Pius XII in 1943 in his encyclical on biblical exegesis, *Divino afflante Spiritu* (1943). This letter has been called in Catholic circles the Magna Carta of scientific exegesis within Catholicism. Not only is the explanation of Scripture according to the rules of modern philology blessed, but an important key to the solution of the conflict between theological and philological exegesis is offered. It is the recognition of the existence of literary genres in the Scriptures. By this recognition the very basis of the nineteenth century efforts is eliminated. As I pointed out earlier, the nineteenth century men thought that every scriptural dictum was reductively a logical statement. It was this tacit and uncritical presumption which had caused all the frustrating confusion in the past. When it was removed, real progress could be made.

From that day on Catholic scriptural studies have gone forward steadily and solidly. During roughly the same time Protestant scholars were moving along the same way. It is not, therefore, surprising that today Protestants and Catholics learn their linguistics, history, and methods in the same schools and under the same masters. Certainly Professor William F. Albright during his days at Johns Hopkins University wielded great influence on the students in his classes in which there were representatives of Catholicism, Protestantism, and Judaism. Albright is a Protestant, but his former students are today holding the chairs of exegesis in Catholic, Protestant, and Jewish centers of theology. In international biblical congresses Catholic and Protestant exegetes meet with no embarrassment and both readily use each other's work. The great Catholic names in recent scripture scholarship, Roland de Vaux, Pierre Benoit, Lucien Cerfaux, Paul Heinisch, Joseph Bonsirven, Stanislas Lyonnet, are not unknown in Protestant circles. In our own English-speaking America, the writings of the two Canadians, Roderick MacKenzie and David Stanley, of Americans like John McKenzie, Roland Murphy, Patrick Skehan, Edward Siegman, Bruce Vawter, and Joseph Fitzmyer are read beyond their own bailiwick.

Can we summarize the orientations followed by these men? I think that broad outlines can be sketched, and for our purpose no more is needed. Their first mark is their complete trust in scientific philology. They confront the text with a great concern for its purity. They are engaged in editorial efforts to present us with a text as genuine as the comparison of manuscripts, quotations, translations, and the newest archaeological findings can supply us. They are all keenly interested in biblical archaeology, and many have worked at it. It is not surprising that the Dead Sea Scrolls occupy so much of their attention. All pursue the study of the languages of the Near East, a scientific enterprise which has made such incredible progress in the last forty years. They are sober in their labors. If the text is not satisfactory, they do not amend it brilliantly in the Bentley fashion. They leave it in the best state possible. Nor do they fill out the lacunae with guesses. They are also making new translations. The French *Bible de Jérusalem* is certainly the most brilliant of all modern vernacular versions, and outside of France the new men are bringing out new translations which are reliable and literate reproductions of the original text in so far as we know it.

At this point it is pleasant to recall what was done in the 1959 meeting of the Catholic Biblical Association of America. It was there proposed, and the proposal was well received, that Catholic and Protestant biblical scholars collaborate to bring forth a modern English version of the Scriptures which would be no revision of any extant translation, and which would then be the one American Bible for Catholics and Protestants alike. I should not dare to prophesy as to the future of this proposal, but it is noteworthy that it was made at all.

The second characteristic of current Catholic biblical study is its holistic approach to the Bible. Today's scholars are not dedicating their time to the analysis of each individual verse. Their aim is total. The individual biblical book must be understood as a whole, and even the book must be understood as one constituent element in the whole constellation which is the Bible. Key ideas are selected and their evolution throughout the process of

Bible-construction is studied. The derivations of the key concepts, the fate of analogous concepts outside of the Bible compilation, the historical circumstances which brought about the evolution of such ideas are all meditated so that the greatest amount of light may be shed on the notion as we find it in our texts today. An evolutionary consideration of the different strands of the biblical message is at work, and in the light of the new work concepts like Covenant, Salvation, Kingdom of God, Faithful Remnant, the Anointed One, the Holy People, Righteousness, Divinity, Man, Sin, and Judgment are being clarified as never before in the history of theology. The Bible is no longer a collection of hundreds of isolated verses. It is one book with a unity of ideas. Isaiah is no longer an object of study isolated from Exodus or the Epistle to the Romans. There is one single evolving message to be found in different stages from Genesis to Revelation, and an understanding of the notion of Trinity is sought for in the Old as well as New Testament.

The third distinctive mark of the new biblical discipline is that it is theological. Historicism has been overcome completely. It is recognized that the Bible deals not with the assignment of the parts of Palestine to the tribes which made up the nomad agglomeration called Israel. If a secular historian wants to use the books for this purpose, that is his privilege; but this is not the concern of the new biblical scholar. In a very true sense, the Bible is not the history of Israel, but rather the story of God's gracious plan to save mankind. It is salvational history and not the history of politics or even ideas.

Much as I rejoice in the progress so brilliantly made by Catholic biblical scholars in the last twenty years, yet as a theologian I have qualms. Of course, it is gladly admitted by any Catholic theologian that the more you know about the Bible, the more you will know about revelation; and that is what the theologian organizes into an intelligent synthesis. But the Bible students show a tendency which would impoverish theology. Unconsciously the scripturists show an impatience with any theology which is not all but exclusively biblical. They have worked hard and well according to their own method, and their efforts have been crowned by an impressive degree of success. Like a young man who has proven his prowess, they seem at times to disdain what was done before they came or by elders of their own time.

The matter has been put most clearly by a Protestant, Walther von Loewenich, and I doubt if any Catholic would go as far as he does. He thinks that scientific exegesis is the only valid way to achieve an understanding of Scripture. A theological interpretation, other than the one indicated by scientific philology, is for him spurious, deriving from and leading to mere mythology. Loewenich thinks that it is the glory and specific task of Protestantism to understand the Scriptures exclusively by the scientific method.

As I have said, it seems impossible for any Catholic to

go so far; and yet there are signs that some Catholic exegetes do move along with Loewenich up to some indefinite point short of his conclusion. For the theologian, Catholic or Protestant, this doctrine is strangling. Granted freely that Scripture has a primacy in theological meditation, yet Scripture simply cannot be the exclusive source from which any worth-while theologian draws.

First of all, there is the matter of tradition. I fully subscribe to the observations of the Lutheran theologian, Jaroslav Pelikan. Tradition is inevitable; it is primitive; it is exegetical. The rabbis before the coming of Christ laid great emphasis on the oral tradition and held it as important as the written word. The writers of the New Testament interpreted the Old according to a Christian tradition which they made normative for the understanding of the Hebrew sacred books. The New Testament itself is a product of tradition, and only in the light of tradition does it have any meaning. What is more, tradition is exegetical. It is positive and negative in its understanding of the sacred page. Certain interpretations are imposed and others are excluded.

Second, I cannot share the current disdain and hostility for Greek or medieval categories in theology. To hear some theologians speak, it is enough to call the other man's thought Greek to expel him and his works into outer darkness. I refuse to consider Greek a dirty word. After all, the Bible itself was written in Greek. Why Hebrew categories, which derive from a people and period of lesser sophistication and smaller speculative inclination, should be superior or more useful than the categories derived from a more reflective culture, deeply engaged in intellectual analysis and synthesis, is for me quite baffling. Actually, I do not think that these lovers of Hebrew modes of thought are in the least enamored of the Hebrew dimension of the message. They are not the least archaic but rather ultramodern, because Hebrew is unwarrantedly considered to be a synonym for existential.

Third, the great contribution of current biblical science is that it has freed us from the incubus of historicism. And yet its descendance from the old historicism brings with it some atavistic traits. The Scripture is not an essay in secular historiography. It speaks of the revealing God. It speaks from faith unto faith. If it is read on some level below faith, then we are engaged in literary antiquities. This can be useful for the theologian, but it is not theology.

The rabbis of Israel and the Fathers of the Church brought forth an exegetical method which has been called mystical, spiritual, or allegorical. In the nineteenth century this kind of exegesis was ridiculed and reviled, mainly because it was not understood. A man accustomed only to historical philology in his encounter with the Bible can only be disgusted when he reads the commentaries of Augustine on the Psalms. But this disgust ought to reveal to that man not a weakness in the Eagle of Hippo but rather in his own digestive apparatus. Augustine was not trying to do what the philologist attempts. Augustine quite honestly and after reflection was convinced that the philological approach would leave the arcana of Scripture wholly undetected. Augustine and his contemporaries looked at the Bible as the word of God. It is not to our purpose here to discuss different theories of inspiration. Let it suffice that for the Fathers the phrase, the word of God, was taken seriously though not childishly.

Augustine saw two dimensions to the biblical affirmation. One was wholly open to the scrutiny of the philologist, and Augustine was anxious to receive his help. But this dimension was not the one which concerned Augustine deeply. There was for him another dimension, where the philologist was quite irrelevant. It was the divine dimension where the word of man was truly the word of God.

Not that Augustine believed that there were two words. There was only one, but it did have two dimensions. The palpable dimension, which is the one to which the philologist restricts himself, speaks either in logical predication or in poetic discourse which uses figures of speech and transferred language. Logic or literary analysis are the proper tools to achieve the content on this dimension.

But the dimension which absorbed the interest of the deeply believing Augustine was the dimension of symbol and ontological analogy. Here the philologist could not assist him. Augustine called on the analogy of faith, the total revelation as it had been communicated to him by the living Church which received him at his second birth. With this guidance Augustine could then see the scriptural human word as a symbolic, sacramental sign pointing to a meaning intended by the revealing God. In consequence, Augustine could see Christology in the musical directions included in the text of the Psalm. Whether Augustine knew that it was, in point of historical fact, a musical director's instruction to a choirmaster, I do not know. He was an acute man and he may well have realized it. However, he did not worry about that phase of it. The words were in the sacred text and they had divine meaning which would hardly be concerned with harps, flutes, and sackbuts.

The symbolic and sacramental nature of the Bible was for Augustine its truest reality. When the Scripture spoke of God as king, Augustine did not worry about the Roman emperor in Byzantium or King David in Jerusalem. He did not think that he would understand God better by making intense studies of the past phenomena of ancient oriental kingship. On the contrary, he felt that he would understand human kings better by knowing that God was above all kings king, and they were kings only because they shared in a phase of divine reality.

The theologian, like Augustine, must be anxious to reach and penetrate this symbolic dimension of the Bible. There he is in touch with revelation which is his field of investigation. The biblical number of stadia between Jerusalem and Emmaus is more than an historiographer's testimony. It has another dimension. The historiographic indication of mileage should be useful for the theologian; but if it were not, he could ignore it.

Now just what is the symbolic dimension of the sacred page? It is the action of God, who is wholly transcendental, whereby He reveals Himself. His self-revelation is not immediate but in a medium, the medium of a verbal expression. He reveals Himself not as a logical truth but as the ontal, or really existent, first truth to be grasped in faith, love, and obedience. The words must not be constrained to act as words do in usual human conversation but in a proportional relationship—the relationship of analogy. When God is called king, we must not equate the predicate with the phenomenon of a human bearer of a crown. The human prerogatives of kings are related to human kings as a certain quality in God is related to Him. Since we do not grasp God in His transcendence, because our minds function on the empirical plane of human experience, that quality can only be grasped in its analogy with the kingly relationship in a human situation. We truly know something about God without having met Him face to face. The knowledge is not the awareness of vision nor yet the mere understanding achieved in the subsumption of realities under conceptual categories. It stands in between. It is more than conceptual knowledge, though it cannot dispense with concepts. It blows up the intuitional factor involved in conceptualization itself. As a result, when the Scripture says God is king, I know that He is so; but in a way far superior, not in degree but in kind, to any human king.

Hence we can only consider childish the remark of some historians of religion who said that the Hebrew writers conceived Yahweh as an oriental despot, that they put a Pharaoh in the sky. To say this indicates a complete lack of sensitivity to communication. When Yahweh was described according to the mean and dreadful trappings of Near East rulers, the meanness and cruelty were all filtered out because the predication was analogous and not logical. Such analogy is not a mere external likeness between God and Pharaoh. The likeness is within. Kingship is better than any human manifestation of it. What Pharaoh wanted to be, and was not, God is.

When the Scripture is considered in this light it speaks to us religiously. There is no need to inquire what kind of wine Noah drank when he became drunk. That makes no difference, and its knowledge would not substantially change the message of God. We are told in a storyteller's way that those whom God has saved still are prone to sin and ignorance. God saves man without changing the human situation. If you wish to call this allegory, I see no objection; but it is not an allegory like Bunyan's *Pilgrim's Progress*. It is quite simply ontological analogy.

Children are prone to be literal when they meet either metaphor or analogy. They substitute an image for a concept. Santa Claus is a jolly old fellow dressed in red with fur trimmings. It takes the children some time to realize that Santa Claus is not a reality as imaged, but rather a theatrical way of saying that one can expect the gracious bounty of unearned giving. As children mature, they feel impelled to go beyond image, and even beyond the univocal content of concepts and terms. They are groping for ontological analogy.

Those who are not accustomed to think about the analogical way of judging will worry about the danger of uncontrolled subjectivism in analogical interpretation.

They need not be. The analogical dimension of the sacred text can only be detected in the light of faith. But faith is not subjective, though it is the action of a subject. Faith is the reaction to a light, and the light comes from the Spirit of God. When the old-fashioned fundamentalist appeals to the inner light in his understanding of the Bible, he is on the right track. The principle is absolutely valid; but I fear that most fundamentalists apply it badly. It must be the Spirit who shows us the analogical dimension of the text, but it must be only the Spirit of God. When we approach the text we must also test the spirit in us, because not all spirits are the Spirit of God.

It is here that the Catholic doctrine of the Spirit is so helpful. The Spirit works in the world through His action in the Church. He is the Spirit of God, the Spirit of Christ, and the Spirit of the *ekklēsia*. Because I am in the Church, the Spirit dwells in me. There is only one Spirit of God. The same Spirit who directs the action and life of the total Church directs me inasmuch as I am in that Church. One is the Spirit and one is His action.

If my biblical understanding is in living resonance with the understanding of the whole Church, then I know that I have read the sacred letter in the light of the Spirit. If my understanding is contradictory to the understanding of the perennial Church, then my light was not from the Spirit of God. It is He who keeps the Church together and it is He who enlightens her in her perpetual function of communicating the Gospel to mankind. Weak though she be in her human structure, she is yet strong by reason of Him who strengthens her. By reason of her presence and operation, I can validly test the spirits.

The action of the Spirit is within. Yet that action makes a visible impress on history. The teaching function of the Spirit is living and throbbing within the Church, and the manifestation of that life is what we call tradition.

Once more we come to the conclusion which current Catholic theology stresses so heavily. Scripture is in the tradition and tradition is in the Scripture. We cannot separate them without losing them both. The union of the living word with the living tradition is a rather nice description of the Church herself.

The spiritual sense of the Scriptures is not in opposition to the philological sense. Both are fused into one reality which is two-dimensional. They are like body and soul. The soul is not the body nor is the body the soul; but the soul acts only through the body and the body lives only by the soul. If the body is neglected, the soul cannot work as it should. A sick man's soul operates in a sick fashion: it can do nothing else. Hence the theologian welcomes with ardor all that the philologist can contribute to the illumination of the biblical text. The more he does, the more he strengthens the body. But if he tells me that there is only a body, or if he unconsciously tends to tell me that, I fear that he is overlooking the essential reality of the thing he is trying to explain. If someone tells me that scientific exegesis—a question-begging label—is the only instrument capable of giving me scriptural meaning, then I can only compare him to a scientist who tells me that anatomy and physiology are the only tools which lead to the understanding of man.

There is an exegesis beyond philological science which is also needed. You can call it theological, mystical, allegorical, or spiritual. I prefer to call it simply ecclesiastical.

Nor is such exegesis static. It grows, and it grows precisely by the new insights of individuals which trigger the awareness of the total Church. The presence of tradition does not hamper the action of the theological exegete any more than gravity hampers the racer. It only keeps him on the ground. In fact, the cry of the Church to all its members is to deepen the awareness of all in the growing explanation of the word of God. The exhortation is to initiative, to evolution, to personal responsibility in the believer's confrontation with God, the author of the book and the savior of the Church.

III

Sacrament and Symbol

There were two men who gave Catholic theology new orientations in the twenties and thirties. They were the French Jesuit, Maurice de la Taille (1872–1933), and the German Benedictine, Dom Odo Casel (1866–1948). They both worked in the field of sacramental theory. De la Taille was interested directly in the Eucharist and Casel was more concerned with the notion of liturgy. The two men went about their tasks in different ways, but their work was complementary. They both dealt with the problem of sacramental sign.

In the light of the subsequent vitality of the liturgical movement what these men had done can be judged as highly significant. It might be profitable to think along the lines they opened up. This would be even more profitable than to reproduce their bare thought. Actually, the value of the work the two men did was not so much in the theories they constructed as in the directions they gave to Catholic theology.

From the second decade of this century to our day there has been vigorous thinking given to the notion and practice of sacrament. Pietism and moralism have been strong currents in Protestantism since the eighteenth century, and something like them can be found in Catholicism as well. Pietism is individualistic and subjective; so is moralism. They can be very energetic and give a warm glow to religious life. Nevertheless, Christianity is a highly social action. Though it can absorb pietism and moralism it certainly cannot be constituted by them. The early Christians were not only called the saints, but they were also known to each other as the brothers; and fraternity implies a society.

Society can worship God only in outward signs and gestures. The individual can pray to God in his heart. The two forms of prayer need not exclude each other; in fact they should not. Yet, given human tendencies, an unnecessary conflict between the two may occur. When this does come about something unsound comes forth. External social prayer may deteriorate into sheer mummery, and internal personal prayer can become an unreal dreamworld of its own.

It was to overcome this needless tendency that genuine liturgy was studied intensely. The carriers of the liturgical movement wished to make of it a public prayer which would also be personally meaningful.

The enterprise is not tricky, but there are those who simply do not like the idea of meeting God in a medium, for a medium means for them either idolatry or delusion.

The medium must of its nature be something material, and if it be put in the place of God then idolatry has taken place. If it is not idolatry, then a power is attributed to it which cannot be its own. The medium, finite and historical, is presumed to channel divine presence. But nothing finite has such power. Hence, mediated contact with God is illusion.

People who reflect in this way want immediate experience of God. If they can achieve this, then they feel free from delusion. Different religions have had their holy men who worked out systems whereby they hoped to bring about the immediate union of man and God. The Indian religions are famous for their efforts, and their complicated systems are structured to bring about the mystical experience. This attempt is not unknown in Christianity, either in its Catholic or Protestant forms.

Yet there seems to be an inner contradiction latent in the efforts. Pure religion recognizes the utter otherness of God and the universal material condition of man. There is a wall of separation between the two, and this wall has been made more impenetrable by man's sinfulness which alienates him still more from the All-Holy.

If the problem is considered in this light, one might despair of any possible communication with God. Yet, the truth of the matter is that we must not so exaggerate God's transcendence that He becomes totally unapproachable, totally distant, without any possibility of intercourse with anything but Himself. After all, the theologies of mankind all insist that in God we live and move and have our being. It was the Hellene Aratus that used those words, but Paul of Tarsus endorsed them (Acts 17:28).

The transcendence of God does not deny His divine presence in all things. It denies only the unmediated encounter between God and man. Those who seek immediate knowledge of divinity with no other powers than those innate in them look in vain. On this side of the eschatological divide man has no right to expect an I–Thou conversation with God.

Yet the whole tenor of the Gospel is that man can have things which he has no right to expect. Man cannot bridge the abyss which separates him from his ground. But God can, and it is the burden of the Christian good news that He is graciously anxious to condescend. But the coming of God will be through a medium. This is the universal law. It must be in a time and in a place, because that is where man is. God can come to man, but man cannot go to God. If God comes, it will be in a temporal and local setting.

In other words, God's visitation is always sacramental. By a sacrament we understand an outward sign signifying a divine approach in benevolence. Every theophany is a sacrament wherein God reveals His personal presence. And every sacrament is a theophany.

Theophanies manifest God's presence in degrees. More of Him can be grasped in one form of theophany than in another. But even in its highest degree the theophany is an historical event, a locus in time and place. This juncture of divine advent with a perceiving man constitutes a sign, for sign is the very heart of theophany and sacrament. We must reflect on the reality of signs.

Much study has been dedicated to signs in the last fifty years. Psychologists have gone into the question with depth and energy. Semanticists have thought much on the matter. Theologians have been wrestling with the problem. In the light of all that has been done we may say something worth-while.

Before we do so, we must make some observations about the position of the antiliturgists. We know the basis of their opposition. They want to reach God in purity, and as a result they wish to eliminate altogether the function of medium, or at least to restrict it drastically. Within Catholicism and Eastern Orthodoxy it is impossible to be an antiliturgist. In both of these churches liturgy is the very substance of worship. The believers may have their inner life of prayer, and they are encouraged to do so; but they are also forced to participate in the liturgy, and from it they achieve godliness. This godliness is enriched by inner prayer and meditation, but it is constituted by sacramental worship.

Within Protestantism opposition to liturgy is possible but not necessary. The rise of the liturgical movement in contemporary Protestant Churches shows quite clearly that the Protestant principle does not exclude liturgical prayer. A priori this must be so. The Protestant principle makes much of scriptural affirmation and the Bible makes much of sacramental sign, especially baptism and the Lord's Supper. What makes antisacramentalism possible within Protestantism is the stress given to the principle of salvation through faith alone. Faith, as many Protestants conceive it, is the experience of being grasped by God. It is empirical and it is a quasi-mystical experience. It is occasioned by the hearing of the word of salvation but not caused by it. In such a vision the holy sign is not an action of God, but rather an act of the believer whereby he witnesses to the congregation that he has been accepted by God in an action anterior to the sacramental process. Strictly speaking, the sacrament is not necessary for salvation. It is only the believer's testimony of salvation to the visible church.

Yet even in this view sacramentalism is latently present. God came to the believer in time and space. God worked on him through temporalities, even if only the medium of the read or preached word. It was in the word that the believer met God. The word is a sign, and in consequence the believer achieved God sacramentally. For the naturalist the world and its manifold elements can mediate divinity; but even for him it is always mediated. In Himself we do not encounter God outside of genuine mysticism.

Hence it is not sacrament to which the antiliturgist objects. He only demands that the sacrament be restricted to one kind of sign, the sign of the word.

Yet the grounds of his opposition are not wise. The big mistake made by many who think about God is that they want to see Him before the eschatological situation. We must cling to the notion that God is utterly other. If we lose sight of this fundamental truth we shall fall into one form of idolatry or other. It is not that man ever really denies the reality of divinity. That he cannot do because divinity is the last dimension of being, and we all are. The ideological Marxist does not deny divinity; he only identifies it with the dynamic *élan* of history. The religious question is never whether we will affirm divinity or deny it, but rather whether we shall identify divinity with the Father whom Jesus revealed. Here man has a choice, but not in the primordial issue of divinity itself.

In the otherness of God we have the divine mystery. That mystery cannot ever be resolved. You simply cannot make God intelligible by the use of the labels which we have discovered for events in history. The human way of knowing is not adequate for the knowledge of God. There is nothing obscurantist about this proposition. It is equivalent to saying that a blind man cannot perceive color; but that does not mean that he can know nothing about color whatever. Color in its concrete reality can excite other kinds of perception. It can activate an angstrom detector; and its registerings can be perceived by the blind man, even though he cannot directly perceive color itself in its proper formality.

God, then, cannot be perceived in His distinctive reality but He can be reached in a medium in which He is present. What will be experienced will be the medium not God. In the sacrament it is the material sign which is empirically achieved; but God is signified, and through that signification we have discovered His presence and operation. This is the universal condition, and it cannot be transcended except in a genuine mystical experience which is itself based on a previous sacramental encounter.

Two corollaries must be drawn at this point in the discussion. First of all, all language concerning God must be symbolic language. The medieval theologians called it description by ontological analogy. The positivist's demand that God be discussed in univocal logical terms is a thoughtless demand. Given the nature of God the positivist's conditions are irrelevant to the discussion. Their method is by definition inept for the task. If the positivist becomes dogmatic and asserts that the positivistic approach is the only valid human search for truth, he becomes absurd. The positivist method cannot justify positivist dogmatism. In fact, it makes it meaningless.

The theologian, then, by the very nature of his enterprise must speak in symbols and analogy. He can do nothing else. It is not a weakness in his effort, but the true fruit of his search.

The second corollary is just as important. Man, in his belief and in his worship, is inexorably involved in symbol, analogy, and sacrament. This universal condition cannot be transcended in the pre-eschatological framework. To restrict the sacramental action to the realm of the spoken or written work is a form of logolatry.

So far I have spoken in general terms, keeping close to phenomenology. It is time to turn to Christian theology. The fundamental belief of all Christians is that God in a series of theophanies revealed Himself gradually and progressively in preparation for the great theophany in Jesus the Christ. In Him revelation was complete and definitive. With Him the last stage of salvational history was inaugurated, and it would last until salvation itself would appear to all at Christ's second coming which will be the flower of His mission.

In Jesus Christ we have the finest realization of the sacramental notion. He was the word of God, not in tittles and jots but in the flesh. He was truly human and truly divine. He, the Son of Man, was the Son of God; he who sees Him sees the Father who was manifested in Him. Here is an external sign manifesting the inward operative presence of God Himself. In Him is the fullness of grace, and of His grace we have all received. This is all ontologically true, but only in faith can it be known.

Christ was not merely the perfect theophany but equally the theophany of the saving God. He was the Savior not only for the men in the days of His sojourn on to death, but for men of all time. Christ must not be conceived of as an isolated event in history. History was itself changed because He abides in it. Men cannot be saved by an absent Christ or a Christ acting by remote control. In Him is salvation; and if He is not here we cannot be saved.

Salvation, like any theological word, is a symbolic term. Theology cannot transcend its symbolic discourse, but it can transpose one symbol to another for purposes of clarification. What then is the meaning of the term, "Christ saves"?

To be saved and to be lost are correlative notions. Historical man had been lost, and that is why he was saved. In what did his loss-condition consist? In his alienation from God. Man's radical desire is to assimilate all reality and be assimilated by it. This can only be done by sharing in the very nature of God who is the transcendental summation of all being. Man needs and unconsciously wants to be divinized. And yet he is only a creature, bent in on his creatureliness through Original Sin.

It was Christ who corrected this situation. In the doctrine of Chalcedon He was a divine person, God of God, Light of Light, true God of true God, and yet He was truly human without that humanity being somehow swallowed up in the divinity. Christ was unconfusedly man and unconfusedly God. In Him humanity was sharing in the divine nature through a unity in person. One was the person, and He divine, but the two natures were unconfused. Here was the perfect ideal for mortal man's sharing in the divine nature, which is the goal of his every striving. Yet the ideal was too high for historical man, who is a human and not a divine person. But the ideal still suggests the pattern of man's divinization. Man is human as Christ was, and if only he can share in Christ's concrete humanity then man is united in Christ to God. This is salvation. It has been described symbolically, but it was described really; not by myth or gnostic allegory.

The pattern of salvation, then, is present; but it is not enough for it to be before our gaze. There is no way in which man by his own powers can take unto himself the humanity of Christ except by some pious fiction resting on velleity. But fictions do nothing on the order of reality. Voluntarism is no solution of ontological problems. Yet, though man cannot take unto himself the humanity of Christ, Christ Himself by divine power can give it to him. This is clearly grace and love.

It is the Christian faith that Christ did just that. He prolonged His stay by communicating His life to His *ekklēsia*, His little flock, His disciples. They would live His life and do His work. He would be in them and they in Him. With a physical body He would go to the Cross and die; but in His resurrection He would take on, in addition, a social body, the Mystical Body of Christ. He would not entirely go away. He would be here in His Church. Like Him and because of Him she would be the great sacrament, human and lowly in her appearance but divine in her inner reality. She would be able to communicate to men the living humanity of Christ in a rebirth. She would continue and apply His saving mission. Only in His name is it given men to be saved, and outside of her there is no salvation.

And it was and is done in liturgical symbolism. Christ, the prime sacrament, acted sacramentally. His life can to some degree be written by an historian, and when this is done, the life and death of a good man is narrated. If the writer has the artist's touch, he will present us with a tragedy. But in the Christian Scriptures and in Christian tradition it was not a human tragedy but a divine comedy. What seems to the historian a tragic death is explained by the early Christians as a saving sacrifice. Now, sacrifice is liturgy and the *leiturgos* is called a priest. The priestly liturgy is also called a mystery, a sacred symbolic action. The first Christian heralds insisted on the liturgical aspect of Christ's death and insisted equally that it was not according to the canons of Jewish liturgy, nor was Christ a priest according to the order of Aaron.

The inspired insight of the New Testament writers makes it clear that for Christian faith Christ acted sacramentally. His life, high-pointed in His passion and death, was God expressing Himself truly but in human symbol. Not the mere symbol of the word but the symbol of liturgical action. Divine condescension spoke to us not only in Christ's *logia* (words) but above all in His *erga* (deeds).

Christ the God-man knowingly and willingly accepted the divine will of the Father, even the death of the Cross. He did so that He might enter humanly into divine fullness, and the result would be that all who shared His humanity, in it and by it would enter with Him into the inner life of the Trinity. He saved humanity, His and that of all those who shared it with Him.

This great truth He conveyed to His own close friends on the night before He died. The early Church remembered the action vividly and made its commemorative renewal the high moment of its assemblies. The proclamation came forth in the guise of sacred symbolic action, in sacrament.

Christ chose for His symbol the most common human action, eating. This quotidian operation is in itself highly significant and mysterious. The little boy who eats the apple becomes ontologically one with the fruit through the process we call assimilation. In this assimilation the apple quite literally becomes the boy, romps with him, cries with him, and laughs with him. Christ by the power of God made Himself truly present in the phenomena of bread and wine, and those who consumed them, according to His own words assimilated His body and blood. Through the symbolic form of eating, Christ shared with His friends His own humanity, the humanity which on the morrow He had willed to give up to God through the ministrations of executioners. Not only did Christ convey His own humanity in His symbol but commanded His own to renew that symbol for others until He should come again.

Symbol is the only way in which God can communicate Himself to men. In symbol men act out the divine design. In symbol the truth is done and the truth is proclaimed. In the light of this truth we can see how literalism is so wearily beside the point. In the baptismal symbol total immersion most vividly portrays the symbolic truth; but since it is symbolic, water is enough without the immersion. He who is washed need not be washed entirely to be symbolically washed wholly.

There is another aspect of symbolism which we must consider. Pigs is pigs, according to rugged common sense, nor has common sense erred in its judgment. Symbols are not products of nature. Things are themselves and they have their own meaning and no other. When a thing means something different from its own being, a mind and a will must give to the thing a new reality. It is by some intelligent act that alien meaning is attached to physical realities. It is by law or convention that the red light at the street corner signifies an order to halt. The red light in its own natural being makes no command. In the same way symbols are only for man. The red light says nothing to a horse, because brute animals do not achieve meaning. Nor would a red light speak to an angel, because by definition angels function on a plane above the material.

A symbol, then, is always the creation of a mind and will. A thinking agent takes what is found in history and gives it a meaning in addition to its own. No amount of laboratory inspection will discover the symbolic nature of a thing. We are told by the old logicians that smoke is a sign of fire. It really is not. Smoke is a consequence of fire, and by analysis of the relation of antecedent and consequent I can infer from smoke to the presence of fire. To be a sign a thing must of itself be some one's intelligence and will say something more than its own reality. As the philosophers say, a sign is not a physical but rather an intentional being.

A symbol is always a sign, but not all signs are symbols. A symbol is a peculiar kind of sign. In the garden variety of signs the signification may be attached to it by arbitrary fiat—as, for example, when a man uses the spoons and forks at table to signify divisions of soldiers in a battle. Generally it is human convention which gives the sign its power to signify something else, and convention makes its signs in terms of similarities between the sign and the signified. Thus, wavy lines on a map can be conventional signs of water because of the wave similarity.

As Paul Tillich has pointed out, a symbol is more than a mere sign, though it is also a sign. When the indicating sign shares in the power and being of the thing it signifies, it is a symbol. There is between the two an analogy, but the analogy is not superficial or imaginative. When you have an imaginative similarity you have a myth. When the similarity is in the being itself by intrinsic ontological analogy then you have a symbol. The thing signified is really present in the symbol, because the sign shares in the being of what it represents.

But we must not forget that a symbol signifies by intent. Any creature is ontologically analogous to God by reason of its being. Yet we must not say that a man is a symbol of God, though he was made to His image and likeness. God must will that a man be a divine symbol, as He did in the case of the kings of Israel.

In divine symbolism the divine intent is free. The natural creature is not by its creation either sign or symbol. In addition to the creative act God must give a new being to the creature, an intentional being, so that it will convey divine meanings through its creatureliness. For man to know God's intent God must reveal it. Hence it is in faith that we recognize symbols and their meaning. Man, either as an individual or as a society, cannot make divine symbols, though he can indeed create religious signs. Sacred symbol and faith go hand in hand. The symbol moves from faith unto faith.

The true divine symbol is like the *Shekinah* of rabbinic thought. The top of Sinai was covered by a cloud of God's presence. The Israelites so recognized it and refused to enter into it because of fear. But their mediator, Moses, entered into the presence and there he could see the back of God. God was present on the mountain in all truth; but His presence was veiled by the cloud, His *Shekinah*. The cloud did more than signify the divine presence; it realized it. God was present in a personal way on the holy mountain, a way unlike to His presence in creation down in the valley. God's presence on the mountain was a saving presence, and His presence at the foot was not saving at all. The *Shekinah*, the *doxa* or glory, are par excellence symbols, God really present but mediated by a visible sign.

That is why the sacramental action of Christ in the Supper of the Lord had first a sacramental effect, and through it the salvation of men. Let us reflect on the symbolism of the symbolical, priestly act of Christ in the Cenacle. In solemn and liturgical expressions He offered tomorrow's death as a human oblation to God. In this sense and only in this sense was the whole action sacrificial. Through the willed symbolism of the phenomena of bread and wine for the purpose of eating and drinking, He shared His humanity with His friends who received the command to do just what He had done until His eschatological return. The participation of the believers in this sacrificial meal included the eating of the blessed food. By it they assimilated Christ symbolically, but still in ontological analogy. By divine condescension each and every one of them became Christ through assimilation. Every time this ritual was in faith renewed the same effect was to be produced.

Now, two things incorporated into the same third thing are incorporated into each other. James the Apostle was so incorporated. So was Peter and so was John. John, Peter, and James are now one with Christ, not by figurative language, not yet in the sense that they shared His purposes by an act of their will. They were really and truly sharers of the body and flesh of the Lord and were in Christ. After the Pentecostal experience this same action took place. The believers who were the *ekklēsia* became the Christ and were His shared living humanity prolonged and extended through space and time. The Church is thus truly though symbolically the Body of Christ. The Church is thus the divine *Shekinah* in the world, just as Christ was. The Church is the Christ symbolically present; and through symbols she, the Christ-symbol, operates. In a change of symbol she is the reality of the Christ-symbol. The Church can only say with St. Paul: "I live now, no not I, but Christ lives in me" (Gal. 2:20).

The Church, therefore, comes forth from the symbolic action of Christ at the Supper and the Cross as the transposed Christ-symbol. In consequence, in symbolic language she hands down to the end of days the Christ-message carried in Christ's human mind which now lives in her. She in symbolic act gives to believers the assimilation into the living humanity of the Lord. She, because of her ontological union with the Saviour, carries on His full human mission: she rules by the kingship of Christ; she sanctifies with holy signs; she suffers and groans to make up what is lacking in the passion of the Redeemer; she heals as did the Lord; she protests against sin and the world in the prophetic spirit of Jesus; she gives unfailing witness to the revelation of God in Christ.

It is only as illuminated by Christ's symbolic action at the Supper and the Cross that we shall understand the

Church. It is only in the symbolic actions of Christ that we shall understand Him. Only in penetrating into this great *Shekinah*, past and present, shall we see the back of God.

Symbolism is the key to good theology. It takes revelation seriously without debasing it. Any essay at literalism brings with it crass misunderstanding. Such misunderstanding will necessarily force the theologians to avoid nonsense and contradiction through any flight from the simplism of treating symbolic language as if it were literal statement. One can then advocate for moralism by treating the whole Gospel as if it were a moralistic exhortation to unselfish virtue with no other message to give. That was done by nineteenth century liberalism. The theologian confronted with an impossible task can abandon his vocation and bury himself in the quasi mysticism of pietism. We saw that in the eighteenth century. The theologian can also consider the revelation of the Gospel, not as a gracious personal intervention of God in history, but as a gnostic allegory explaining existence, reality, and the unknown god. That perhaps is the temptation of our day.

The doctrine of symbolism and symbolic sacrament is not esoteric cultism nor magic hocus-pocus. It is the conclusion of the truth that God is transcendent and yet comes to man. It is not mythology whereby images are spun out merely as pointers to a truth which must be grasped in some other form of knowledge. It is not esoteric communication intelligible only to the adepts. It rests on the notion of the analogy of being, and even though Karl Barth called that insight the invention of Antichrist, it is a rather godly conception.

Aristotle made simple rules for inference. One of the rules was that the *logos* must be strictly such. A term must not be used *ana logon*, up to the category, but it must be *kata logon*, strictly according to the category. These ideas were expressed by Latin logicians as terms which were either univocal or equivocal, and under the latter class Aristotle placed the analogous term.

Aristotle laid down good rules for inference but he restricted the field excessively. In the Academy of Plato, where Aristotle had gone to school, mathematicians like Eudoxos went far beyond the logic of Aristotle. They saw that there were proportional relationships or, as they called them, analogies. In this sense the medieval masters used the word analogous. They meant by it the validity of applying terms to subjects, not absolutely but proportionally. A half of a plum in no sense is equal to half a watermelon, but it is proportionally equivalent. If the term proportionally predicated is really verified in the subject we have an intrinsic ontological analogy. If it is not intrinsically verified but is only a transferred use of image the analogy is literary and extrinsic.

The medieval scholars found the idea of intrinsic analogy a worth-while insight. It could tell us much of an object which I could not directly perceive but whose reality was shared proportionally by something which could be perceived. My knowledge of the unperceived would not be direct nor in the rigor of the category, but proportional knowledge would be achieved. I would know something and not merely nothing. Of course, this whole concept rests on the notion that all being is one because one being is absolute, knowable only by analogy, and all others are beings by participation. This view is the only one compatible with the absoluteness of reality within a manifold of being.

Barth rediscovered for himself with vividness the transcendence of God. He is loyal to his vision and is afraid that he may lose it if he admits a doctrine of participation. His fear is needless. Not only can he use the notion, but I am afraid that neither he nor any one else can long think without it.

If we believe in the transcendence of God and the participation of all things in God's being, then the doctrine of symbol and sacrament is already in principle built up for us.

IV

Ecumenism and the Roman Catholic Church

The ecumenical movement is both an idea and an historical fact. The idea in its abstract purity is simple enough; it is an invitation to the churches professing faith in Jesus Christ to come together in the hope that in some future day they will all be one. The coming together is the immediate goal of the idea. The final union is a desired consequence. It is very important to keep these two facets distinct. As so many voices within the historical movement have declared, the final union of the churches must be God's work, exercised in His good time. The coming together is man's work, not indeed without God's grace, yet always with a human appeal to man's action founded on divine trust.

Keeping these distinct elements in mind, ecumenists will not lose courage if their efforts do not quickly achieve the consequence for which they hope. If they can bring the churches together to hold dialogue, their purpose has been achieved and they need not be disheartened. The rest lies in the hands of God, whose will the ecumenist will accept with faith and obedience.

Much has been written about the ecumenical idea. There is no reason why more need be said in the present context. It is better to consider ecumenism as an historical fact in order to give suggestions for a more effective effort.

As a matter of fact the ecumenical movement which we know is the fruit of Protestant inspiration. It is equally a matter of fact that there is ecumenical activity within the Roman Catholic Church. One need only point to the Una Sancta Association in Germany which is Catholic in its origins and existence, though it calls itself interdenominational and at the recent Eucharist Congress in Munich held meetings with Protestant speakers on its program. Likewise Dr. Willebrands of Holland directs the Catholic Conference on Ecumenical Questions. More names and societies could be mentioned but it does not seem necessary for our purpose. Yet if all these groups be lumped together, they will not compare impressively with the World Council of Churches, which, because of its size and importance, is the first thing one thinks of when the word ecumenical movement is heard.

Now the World Council as a matter of fact is dominantly Protestant. There is of course a non-Protestant sector in its fellowship. Different Eastern Orthodox churches belong to it, but the great Slav churches have only now seen their way to enter into it formally. It must also be observed that the Orthodox influence in the Council is somewhat ambiguous.

As for the presence of other non-Protestant churches in the Council, one can only say that it should be gratifying to the Council that they have joined. But their presence and contribution have not been highly significant. Far more significant for the work of the Council is the *absence* of the Roman Catholic Church than the co-operation of its own non-Protestant members.

It seems clear enough that the Roman Catholic Church is a grave problem for the ecumenists of the World Council of Churches. If it came to pass that all Christians except the Roman Catholics entered into unity—in today's atmosphere a very sanguine hypothesis—less than half of all Christian believers would be united into that one church. That church, large as it would be, would be smaller than the already united Roman Catholic Church. In such an event, instead of a multitude of Christian churches, there would be only two. From the point of view of the ecumenical hope, that would still be one church too many. Yet from the point of view of the ecumenical effort, it would be a consoling event even though ecumenical impulse would not be definitely satisfied.

The Real Structure of the Problem

It is not my intention to solve the problem which Roman Catholicism presents to the World Council ecumenists. Instead I shall try to find the real structure of the problem, lest it be simplified falsely or misconstrued exaggeratedly.

Of course the Roman Catholic Church does offer a solution to the World Council. It is a well known one and obvious. It takes the form of the advice that all Christians become Roman Catholics. The result naturally would be a single church. But it is equally well known that this counsel is unacceptable to the overwhelming majority of non-Catholics.

The reaction of non-Catholic ecumenists to the Catholic solution is varied. There are those who see in the Protestant Reformation the divine rescue of the true gospel after the Catholic Church's almost total corruption of it. For such thinkers a return to Catholicism with its implied rejection of the reform is sacrilege. In all conscience they cannot tolerate the notion of becoming members of a church which to them is apostate and perverse.

Others do not feel any strong compulsion to be loyal to the Reformation. They are willing to see in it a well-intentioned movement which smothered itself in the ambiguities of history. But they feel this is also true of the continuous history of the Roman Church. As they see it, the moment calls for loyalty neither to the reform nor to unreformed Catholicism. Both are wrong and both contain elements of truth. A serene study of the ancient sources and the insights of the living churches can bring about a better formula than either the Protestant Reformation alone or Catholicism alone. Both Protestants and Catholics must give and take.

There are even a few voices which sound as if church unity were merely a matter of will. If all the churches have a good and sincere will toward union, making this goal the high point in their strivings, union can be achieved now. It is only willful stubbornness which keeps the churches apart. For these spirits the Roman Catholic Church is the most stubborn of all, un-Christian and unreasonable in her counsel and demands.

One can also detect a few Protestant ecumenists who would be willing to have their churches enter into the Catholic Church but they insist that the Catholics must give better conditions than those offered today. It might be that in the future such a relaxation of demands on the part of the Roman community will take place. Then in principle there is no reason why Protestants could not solve the ecumenical impasse by becoming Catholics.

All these attitudes can be found among Protestant ecumenists but perhaps the dominant feeling among them is a pained impatience with Catholic aloofness. This impatience, in most cases, however, does not make for anger (though in a few cases it does). The impatience resigns them to go on without the Roman Catholics, but still leaves the door wide open to the Catholics to join them in their efforts.

Now Catholics are not ignorant of these various reactions of Protestant ecumenists. Likewise Rome has manifested respect and sympathy for the ecumenical ideal pursued by non-Catholic Christians. The present Pope has made this quite clear. If this is so, how can we explain the consistent refusal to collaborate formally and officially with the World Council? (There *is* some unofficial and informal co-operation.)

As the Protestants see it, it cannot be the ecclesiology of Roman Catholicism. That is not much different from its counterpart in Eastern Orthodoxy, and the Orthodox have found it possible, in spite of it, to take active part in World Council ecumenical action. The Orthodox have implicitly and explicitly affirmed that only their church is the true Church and the problem of disunion can be met validly only if all the other churches become Orthodox. This makes no deep impression on the Protestants who hear the message but they are more than willing to have the Orthodox members of their union say it. Any annoyance in non-Orthodox circles seems slight and there appears to be sincere gratitude that the Orthodox speak their mind *within* the framework of the World Council rather than outside of it. At least they are in it and have shown charity to this degree. Cannot the Romans do at least as much?

Doctrine Does Divide the Churches

We have been told, and truly, that it is more than doctrine which divides the churches. No one can deny the validity of the observation. But it is just as true to state that doctrine does divide the churches. It is even more significant that the attitude to doctrine is at the present moment more divisive than doctrine itself. For some Christians doctrine is the basic question which confronts ecumenical comparison. It is not secondary nor can any progress be made until this first question is solved. Others think that the matter of doctrine is indeed important but still secondary. Union can be achieved by exploring areas outside of the field of doctrine, where one can find strong footholds which will bring the churches together effectively. When they are thus united doctrinal difficulties will tend to melt away. There are still others who find the whole discussion of doctrine distasteful and believe that it should be ignored altogether in our labors to make the many churches one. Is it mere blindness to think that the second and third groups are growing larger in World Council discussions while those of the first group are constantly diminishing in influence and numbers?

Now we have seen that the Roman Catholic Church is no foe to the ecumenical enterprise, for there are ecumenical associations within it. We have also seen that this same Church is not at all hostile to the World Council of Churches, for Catholics in good standing unofficially, but quite really, do work with it. Why, then, unlike the Eastern Orthodox churches, will the Roman Church on principle refuse to join it? It is easy to say that it is because of pride and arrogance, but the very ease with which this can be said is itself a good ground for suspecting that this is not the answer. The truer answer is that the vision which the Roman Catholic Church has of herself will not permit it logically or psychologically. This statement holds for the present moment and for the

World Council as it now is. If the form of World Council were to change and if another day were to bring a profoundly different configuration of the total ecumenical effort, it is not inconceivable that the Catholic Church might become a member. But concerning such vague and undefined contingencies nothing valid can be said now.

A Roman Catholic Self-Evaluation

It would be silly to ask non-Catholics to share the Catholic Church's view of herself but it would be disastrous if they were not to know it. If we are to speak to each other, we should know how each partner of the conversation appears to himself. It is antecedently thinkable that the partner in dialogue is in error in his self-evaluation but it is unthinkable that the intercourse would be fruitful if we did not take such self-evaluation into account.

The Roman Catholic Church (and therefore each Catholic to the degree in which he is assimilated into the genuine life and being of his Church) believes that this Church is exclusively the Church of Christ. By that fact she believes that she is Christ continued in space and time, with His mission to save, to teach, to judge, to comfort, to guide, to sanctify, and all this she will do because Christ and Catholicism are fused into one life with Him as head and she as the body. Because she believes that His name saves and in no other name is there salvation, she conceives of herself as the saving instrument of God for men, and in her view there is no other. She well knows that God in his soul-loving benevolence also brings men who are non-Catholics to a happy term by uncovenanted mercies. But in this saving act, such souls are attached invisibly to the visible Church. We cannot call them members, but they are truly adherents. No man can say who or how many they are, nor is that man's concern. The Roman Catholic Church must continue in the function given to her: to preach the Gospel, dispense the grace-giving sacraments, scold the slothful, protest against iniquity and sin, especially when they are at work within the Church herself. (She knows all too well that sin plays a heavy part in her own life.) If God in His love is willing to give the graces, which He entrusted to her in such a way that they are really hers, to those beyond her visible unity, there is no resentment but only joy and gratitude. In this divine act there is no contempt of the church nor a bypassing of her. God is only making up by His omnipotence for the finitude of the Church's efforts. It is God aiding His Church in her mission to save souls. But no other instrument is ordained by God to dispense grace to mankind.

This is the theory and spirit of Catholicism. It may appear utterly preposterous to a non-Catholic, but there it is. Psychologically and logically the Roman Catholic Church simply cannot conceive of any other human union as ordained by God to mediate salvation, even though individual members of such a union be in grace. Such grace is immediately given by God in favor of this individual. God can use the individual's religious union and its acts as occasions to give grace to the individual, for in non-Catholic groups there are always *vestigia ecclesiae*, vestiges of the Church, though the separated unions themselves are neither the Church nor part of it. They can be occasions for salvation but they are not ordained instruments thereof.

A council of churches not in union with the Roman Church is at the outset a misnomer from the Catholic's point of view. He considers them something less than churches. Psychologically he gags at the idea of Christian Churches which are not Roman Catholic. His intelligence tells him not to be scandalized by verbalism, but emotions defy reason. In conversations under the auspices of such an organization of which a Catholic might be a member, he would find himself perforce doing what to him seems very wrong. He would have to entertain seriously postulates on the part of his partner in conversation which are a denial of the very basis of his Catholic faith to which he is totally committed. For the sake of the dialogue he would have to listen to positions and theories which in his own history have long ago been definitely rejected. All this he would have to do in seriousness and unfeigned love. This is more than most men can do. For the Catholic it would be especially difficult because he thinks that doctrine is all-important and that it is unchanging. When he came to realize that he was almost the only one with this conviction, the dialogue would be for him absolutely frustrating.

Nor is the situation of the Eastern Orthodox churchmen really parallel to that of the Catholics. They already have tolerance for widely diverging views within their own sisterhood of churches. The concept of autonomous regional churches, loosely bound together by common rites, common creedal formulae, and common customs, is a much thinner idea of unity than that obtaining in Catholicism. Their Principle of Economy can lead them to accept as valid positions and institutions which Catholics would reject. Even now, with all these differences, there are Eastern Orthodox churches who take part in World Council affairs with some misgiving and reluctance because they feel that their participation is somehow contradictory to their being. If this is felt by the Orthodox, imagine the condition of a Roman Catholic!

Needed: Catholic-Protestant Conversations

Does this then mean that the Protestant must resign himself to the bleak picture of working ecumenically without any future encounter with his Catholic brother? I think not. There is even now the very practical possibility of holding ecumenical conversation outside of the framework of the World Council. This possibility is not attractive to the Protestant, especially if he is closely connected with the Council and its genesis. The Council represents the high point of all Protestant ecumenical endeavor and progress. The Protestant would think it sheer treason to something which under God's inspiration has already brought about greater union and promises yet more. To abandon it in whole or in part just to please Catholic sensitivities would appear to the Protestant folly and sin.

Any non-Catholic ecumenist, because of his commitment, should want to speak to Roman Catholics. The World Council is by profession and in deed an ecumenical enterprise. The Council does not identify itself with the Church of Christ but wishes to be a ministering agency for all the churches in order that the Spirit may inspire them to ever greater unity. The Council wishes to be a servant and not a master, a means and not an end. We all know the human tendency for some agency, originally devised to solve a certain problem, slowly to become an end in itself, developing its own importance and clinging to its own structure. The World Council will not escape the influence of this tendency common to all human organizations. In order to be true to its own idea it will be imperative that it frequently examine its own conscience and be anxious to further its own work by using new means for its purpose, even when such means seem revolutionary. It must foster and foment conversations between separated Christians even if this be done according to a pattern not yet used. The Council is well aware that its house is not congenial to the Roman Catholic for the reasons we have already seen. Could it not, then, true to its own purpose, help to arrange Catholic-Protestant or Catholic-Orthodox meetings, under auspices other than its own, where the tacit assumptions of World Council members would not be the unspoken rules of discourse?

Catholic ecumenical groups would gladly enter into such meetings and they would be highly profitable. Much work has been done in the last fifty years which makes it possible and pleasant for Catholics and non-Catholics to come together and ventilate their ideas. The old shibboleths which worked like a red flag on an irritated bull have lost their exciting power. *Sola Fides, sola scriptura,* are phrases which the Catholic is willing to accept, if they are understood in the light of Catholic principles. These slogans no longer terrify. In the last fifteen years there have been many conversations between Catholic and Protestant theologians, between Orthodox and Catholic thinkers, and all are pleasantly surprised how much agreement can be found in areas where all presumed there would only be divergence. Both sides had previously misconstrued the intent of certain axiomatic formulas used by the other party. The old Cyprianic phrase, outside of the Church there is no salvation, is just as Protestant as Catholic. The Protestant merely locates the Church in a locus other than the Catholic. On the application of the axiom there will be true conflict, but not on the principle itself.

And so it goes with so many other formulas. The clearing up of confusion and the recognition of the multiplicity of dimensions in hallowed terminology brings soothing light to all partakers in the colloquy.

Catholic ecumenists ask a special charity and consideration from non-Catholic ecumenists. If I plan a love feast to entertain my Jewish friend, my friendship is shortsighted if all the dishes on the table are such that the Jew cannot partake of them by reason of his own religious commitments. My love feast will be a harrowing occasion for him and rouse in him the suspicion that his very

Jewishness is consciously or unconsciously under attack. This is no way to make friends and influence people.

The Virtue of Patience

Above all, Catholic and Protestant ecumenists must develop the virtue of patience. Centuries of hostility have colored our attitudes toward each other and we cannot see simply what is simply there. Each member of the dialogue must keep on learning, keep on revising his concept and image of his partner in high talk. Misunderstandings cannot be avoided for some time to come but we must not harden the misunderstandings which the past has forced on us.

The one thing we must all remember is that the purpose of the Ecumenical Movement is conversation. Its hope is one Church, but the hope is not the humanly projected teleological goal. Hence the ecumenical obligation is to promote colloquy. To promote it we need to do more than merely be ready for it. We must with patience and forbearance overcome the difficulties which stand in the way of meeting. If my friend is embarrassed when in my house I shall hold converse with him elsewhere. The conversation is important, not the place where it is to be held.

V
Revelation, Dogma, and Theology

Religion is a human thing. It is a reaction of man to the ultimate dimension of reality. That dimension the Greeks called *to theion*, the divine. There can be good religion and bad—but there will always be religion. This is true for a society and true for the individual. Man's choice is not between godlessness and god-seeking. He is born a god-seeker. His choice is between true worship and idolatry.

This is made clear for us, in our day, by the social and economic system called Communism. It prides itself on being atheistic. But it merits this adjective only if the word is understood to mean that the ultimate is not personal after the fashion in which the Judeo-Christian religions have conceived it. It does not merit the adjective if it is understood to be a denial of the ultimate dimension of reality. Communism has its ultimate: the basic power in the universe which acts as a matrix for all action and evolution. This power is highly dynamic in Communism nor is it capricious. It produces the evolution of all things unto ever higher stages of the co-ordination of the forces which are rooted in it. This motion is inexorable. No man and no group of men can thwart this basic élan in all things. The power is conceived as benevolent because it is moving reality in a fashion which satisfies the desires of man. The evolution passes through the dialectic of affirmation, negation, and synthesis. Yet each synthesis brings the universe nearer to the beatific state foreshadowed by the longings of the human heart.

This total scheme is a theology, the fruit of rational reflection on the ultimate dimension of the real. It is a natural theology because the tacit postulate is that all being is homogeneous. Hegel worked out a similar theology, but he supposed that the true index of being was its spirituality. All things were homogeneous with ideas. Karl Marx accepted the same structure of thought, but said that all beings were homogeneous with the unthought object of experience.

In Marxism we note three things. The first is a perception of the ultimate as it unveiled itself to Marx's gaze. Marx operated on the postulate that he *saw* reality as it really is. There was a startling illumination at some point in his life. He then formulated the intellectual content of this experience in a number of genuine Marxist propositions. He and his followers developed and are still developing these basic propositions into an ever fuller rational scheme which wishes to explain reality and offer a solid foundation for good action.

What makes Christianity and Marxism opposing visions

is the fact that they are religions relying on contrary revelations. Christianity and mathematics are not opposed things, because mathematics is not at all concerned with the absolute. They are generically different things. Marxism and Christianity in their roots are specifically the same and they are contraries—*contraria sunt eiusdem speciei* (contraries are specifically the same). Marxism and Christianity must ever be opponents because they cannot but express themselves in contrary propositions. They start with opposing visions of the divine, which is the ultimate dimension of reality.

Christianity is based on the Hebraic perception of divinity. For the Christian, Christianity is Israel fulfilled. For the Jew, Christianity is Israel perverted. But for both, Christianity is an affirmation of Israel and of the substantial legitimacy of its theology.

For both Christian and Jew, the Ultimate in condescension approached man in a personal, immaterial encounter. In that encounter the Ultimate revealed itself as in a conversation between two persons. The likeness was not thorough, but only the analogy of friendly conversation could express it adequately, even though imperfectly.

Marx believed that by purifying man's perceptive powers he could achieve the Ultimate in its relevant significance. Jews and Christians believe that the valid knowledge of God comes not through the initiative of man but through God's gracious initiative. God freely reveals Himself because He loves man. Without this self-revelation the mystery of the Ultimate remains densely opaque. Revelation will not remove the mystery but it does permit man to see divinity as in a glass darkly.

Revelation is the starting point for Christian life and thought. Acceptance of revelation is free on the part of man. For the Christian there was a whole chain of theophanies from the beginning of the human race until the definitive revelation of God, whom the Hebrews called Yahweh, in Jesus Christ.

Revelation is symbolically called the Word of God. This must not be taken naïvely because God does not communicate by words. But in the revelatory encounter God does communicate truth, truth concerning divinity in as far as it is relevant to man's salvation. This revelation must be given to some man who will achieve it in a wordless intuition which works like consciousness where no concepts are involved. If the man who has thus received revelation is commissioned to transmit it to others, then we call him a prophet, a spokesman of God. He will not convey the revelation in the wordless fashion in which he himself achieved it. He will use human words which evoke human concepts. Those who hear him or read his message are now in possession of revelation, but they have acquired it mediately and not immediately as the prophet did.

Words and concepts are of the finite order. They are formed for human needs in man's contact with the myriad facets of the universe. The transcendental God lies beyond such meeting and therefore the words and concepts are not univocal designations of God or of the divine action in history, because they were born for an entirely different task. Yet all things bear likeness to God, and the prophet will use words and concepts by which in terms of likeness but not of direct vision, we can grasp the saving truth of divinity.

The prophets are few and the great prophet, Christ, is unique. The overwhelming majority of men meet revelation through prophetic communication. Even in such communication more than words are used, though they are also used. The prophet's gestures, allusions, insinuations, and vital references are parts of his communication. The communication comes forth in more than words. Part of it was not verbalized and in fact verbal expression will never exhaust the communication no matter how many verbal formulae are framed to do so.

As time separates the believer from the prophet, between the prophet and the man of faith there is a carrier of the prophet's revelational message. This is the living Church. Yet the Church is not merely a continuous human society which can carry attitudes and discoveries of the past. This is the way culture is transmitted. But human societies do not transmit the past accurately. They are always modifying the original content so that quickly or slowly they change its original texture. The same cannot happen in the Church because its structure is different from the structure of secular society. It is a living body in which the Holy Ghost is the permanent soul keeping the body of Christ identical and the same. The vision of Christ, due to the power of the Spirit, remains in the Church intact. She shares ever in the prophetic experience of the Word made flesh. From the living Church the believer receives the genuine, uncontaminated, and incorrupt revelation. In quasi-substantial unity with her the Spirit lives out His mind so that the revelatory moment is constantly reborn in those who adhere to the Church.

Revelation is principally unverbalized even when words are used to mediate it. The revelation, the abiding possession of the Church in her union with the living Lord, must be mediated in language because this is the social nature both of the Church and of man. The mediating function belongs officially to the hierarchy but the hierarchy shares its mission with all Christians. Hence the communication through language is actually performed by all the faithful but always under the direction and control of the hierarchy which is the episcopate. This control is exercised by the bishops by comparing all doctrine with the two instruments of the episcopate, Scripture and tradition. These things are not over the Church but tools in the hands of the bishops. Nor are they really two in their actual existence. Tradition includes the Scripture and Scripture comes to life in its fusion with tradition.

Scripture is a gracious gift of God to the Church. It is a human set of writings, but all were written under the guiding and determining inspiration of the Holy Ghost. It is the living word which carries God's message and the written dead letter takes on life in the living tradition. Tradition is the formal teaching of the hierarchy. It takes on many forms. The highest and most effective form is the solemn pronouncements of the defining episcopate.

Catholics and the Orthodox will agree that this happens in ecumenical councils. They will disagree on which episcopal meetings are ecumenical. Catholics also see the defining episcopate acting in the definitions of the Roman Pontiff in whom resides the plenitude of episcopate in which all other bishops participate and which the other bishops possess *in solidum* but only by participation with the Roman bishop. On this point the Orthodox will have very serious reservations.

When the episcopate speaks in its plenipotentiary capacity, revelation is verbally defined. Such definition is now a dogma. There are other teachings of the same episcopate which are not proposed in the form of definition but are yet the faithful communication of the revelation of Christ. The whole Church accepts these teachings and rightly so. There is no need for every phase of the revelation to be delivered in a solemn fashion with the consequence that its nonreception be the cause of excommunication. Only in times of confusion and danger will teaching be given in this way. For the ordinary needs of the Church, the bishops speak in the ordinary way of life and action. Where there is a consensus of such doctrine, manifested in the consensus of the believing people of God, we have the true revelation as taught by the Church universal which is defended from error by the indwelling Spirit.

Hence the revelation, always exactly preserved in the living Church because of the stimulating and preservative influence of the indwelling Spirit on the solemn teaching of the hierarchy, brings forth dogmas. The dogma is not the revelation in its original status. It is the verbal expression of it. It is also a very precise formulation in the light of a special historical context. Dogma permits evolution, though revelation does not. That is given once for all and totally delivered forever to the saints (Jude, 3). Dogma, the verbal expression of that revelation, will undergo more and more clarification as the times need it. The Church, through its teaching organ, the episcopate, must evolve its own dogmas so that they can be rightly understood without the danger of misleading the faithful who learn from the hierarchy. True, all believers share in the indwelling action of the Spirit who is the inner teacher of the Church. From the teachers the believing body of the faithful learn and receive the Church's message. As St. Paul says, not all are teachers.

Revelation and dogma are thus related to each other as God's communicated truth and the ecclesiastical verbal formulation of it. Such expression is always exact for the purpose of the communication. Beyond dogma there is yet another teaching, the ordinary teaching of the magisterium, which is no less valid than dogmatic pronouncement but which is not expressed with the same rigorous demand. It is still in the process of final and accurate expression. It does not usually need such precise formulation because its possible ambiguities do not offer a threat to the unity and orthodoxy of the Church.

The Church is a union of men. Christ and the Spirit belong to this union formally, but all other members are human with all the Adamic complexity of humanity. Some men are moved to use their intelligence not only as a tool for creating the conditions for a satisfactory life but also as a contemplation of truth for its own sake. These men are of great value to the community though their work is not "practical." All advances in living together rely on the discoveries these men make. Esthetics, morality, and pure science are not, by their formal structures, practical studies but practical arrangements in society derive in great part from the work of men engaged in these disciplines. Revelation is for salvation but it is primarily a message of truth. It is not surprising, then, that in the Church there will be Christians, who like scientists in other fields, dedicate themselves to the contemplation of the truth of revelation, and they will do so because they are interested in the truth for its own sake. These men are called theologians.

The theologian is not the appointed teacher of the faithful. Only the bishop and those whom he sacramentally assimilates into his own task can enjoy the teacher's title. Of them we do not demand scientific dexterity. They need only deep resonance with the revelation carried by the Church and a humble loyalty to the Spirit who keeps the revelation constant and pure in the total Church. From these teachers the theologian learns both revelation and dogma. By accident the teacher may be a theologian but this is not necessary nor is it usually the case. There are not too many Basils and Augustines in the ranks of the hierarchs, while simple priests, deacons, and laymen have been outstanding theologians. The title D.D., which all Western bishops receive with their episcopal consecration, is honorary and yet just, for they in the first place are the official teachers of divinity for their churches.

The theologian's task is a scientific one. He will use the method of dialectical intelligence on the data of revelation. He does so in order to make the best and most economic use of intelligence on the object of his faith. Hence theology has been rightly called the science of faith or in the classical phrase of St. Anselm, *fides quaerens intellectum*, faith in search of intelligence.

The theologians from the beginning accomplished their task in the same generic way. Specifically, individuals move differently but the genus of operation is identical. The first theological task is to achieve the revelation. The definitive expressions for certain phases of the revelation are dogma. Hence the theologian is always guided by the dogmatic pronouncements of the episcopate. These declarations do not by any means cover the whole range of revelation. For the elements not touched by dogmatic decrees the theologian will go to the teaching hierarchy working in its ordinary way. The two tools which the hierarchy ordinarily uses are Scripture and tradition. Nor need we reject the Protestant formula, Scripture alone, provided we understand the phrase to mean the Scriptures kept alive by the enveloping living tradition.

In consequence of this primary task, the theologian must begin by using the Scriptures. Here we run into a difficulty. There are those who wish to use the biblical communication with no other approach than the science of philology. This science is naturalistic and cannot, by its own chosen limitation, touch the supernatural dimension of the books. If this method makes its own limitation a negation of the existence of the supernatural, we are no longer dealing with the theology of the Church. Theology welcomes all the philological work the scientific exegete can bring to bear on the text. There just cannot be too much of it. Even though the supernatural element interests the theologian more, still the natural dimension of the writings is so closely connected with the supernatural depth of the message, that light on one necessarily brings light to the other. Yet it remains true, as the earlier theologians have shown by their work, that philological penetration of the text is *ad bene esse* of the theological enterprise but not simply *ad esse*.

The orientation with which the theologian of the Church goes to Scripture is always the orientation of tradition. From tradition he knows what books constitute the Bible. From tradition he knows how the Church has understood the Bible. Only from tradition does he know that the Bible is the word of God. Tradition therefore is the basis of the theologian's investigation.

Where will he find it? First of all in the historical statements of the total episcopate. This means the doctrine of all ecumenical councils. The Catholic theologian will also include under such statements the *ex cathedra* definitions of the popes. After them he will study carefully the writings of the Fathers, those theologians venerated by the first eight centuries of the Church. These have always been accepted as true voices of the valid tradition. However, it is the consensus of the Fathers rather than the ideas of any one of them which manifests the tradition of the Church. Individually they are not inerrant but in their collectivity they give us the orthodox doctrine of the Church.

If the consensus of the Fathers holds this high place, by the same token the consensus of later theologians is authoritative. In many respects this consensus, though not so venerable, can be more useful than patristic doctrine, for it deals with questions more relevant to our day. The practical problem in studying this phase of tradition is that it is no easy thing to ascertain just what is the consensus of these many men. Yet the principle is clear enough, though its application is difficult.

Tradition shows up most dramatically in the official worship of the Church, the holy liturgies. These were authoritatively imposed on the faithful by the hierarchy, and though their main function is to address the Church to God, yet they indirectly teach the faithful the truths of God. It is not without reason that the Nicene Creed is a formal part of the liturgies both Eastern and Western. Once more we must look for the consensus of the liturgies and always remember that the language and action of communal prayer is not a theological expression of faith.

Nor must the theologian overlook the doctrine implicit in the different canon laws of the Church, which, though they are directed toward the external action of the Christians, yet imply doctrinal positions. In like manner the tranquil faith of the living people of God, as manifested in their spontaneous art, spontaneous devotion, spontaneous religious language and customs, also show forth the orthodox tradition of the Church. Here it is very difficult to find consensus and most theologians shy away from the task precisely because of its hardships. It is clear that the theologian is much concerned with history and historical events. He must go to the lived past and to the living present. This requires a wide understanding and it is no easy thing. Yet, easy or hard, it must be done if theology is to stay healthy and lively. If it is not done, theology degenerates into a walleyed concentration on some little corner of the total theological field with no relevance to current concern.

The theologian wants to bring together the doctrine of tradition found in all these sources. The elements are countless and of themselves do not appear as a unity. Hence the theologian must use some kind of synthesizing principle. It will always be derived from some kind of philosophy. Now the theologian is not a philosopher even if he uses philosophical principles for his work. The point is that he just uses philosophy and the justification of his action is that it is useful. Catholic theologians from the ninth century onwards have gradually formulated a philosophy which they think gives the theologian a good tool for his work of synthesis. But it must be remembered that the theologian considers philosophy as ancillary to his proper work. Philosophy is a handmaiden but not the mistress.

This outline of the theologian's action is best seen in what is called systematic theology. However, it can produce subordinate pursuits. We hear much of biblical theology and patristic theology. Today there is a deep interest in liturgical theology. These names are a little bit ambiguous. They may mean the exclusive use of these sources in the erection of a systematic theology. There is certainly a place for such theology but it will always be inadequate. No one source alone gives us all of tradition. The names may also mean an historical study of the theology implied in the Bible or in one or more Fathers or in some particular liturgy. This kind of work is history rather than theology, though the theologian is the best man to do it.

This brings up the question of mystical theology. Again we run into an ambiguity. The phrase may mean the rational study of the mystics recognized as such by the tradition of the Church. Such study would express in theological concepts the implicit doctrine in mystical writings. It would be just as rational a theology as the most philosophical treatise on divinity. It can be a most fruitful investigation and one not too common in Christian history.

On the other hand, if we mean, by mystical theology, an understanding of Christian doctrine mainly or exclusively achieved in the experience of prayer and piety, I would not call this theology at all. It is the deepening of the meaning of faith not through concepts but in the ineffable communion of God with an individual soul, and this is prayer. This is obviously a wonderful thing, much to be desired, better than theology, but just because it is better it is not theology. Intellectualism is the heart of theology, just as mysticism is the heart of the soul's full achievement of God. Theology moves from faith as given by God through his Christ in the Church. Mysticism moves from an ineffable experience given by God to an individual soul. Theology and mysticism are different activities which are completely friendly to each other but which cannot be considered identical.

Is theology, then, a dedication which is only a matter of personal satisfaction, unrelated to the whole Church? Not at all. The theologian of the Church works for the Church. He exercises an ecclesiastical function. Not every believer has to be a theologian but theologians are needed by the Church. For this reason the Church has always considered the theologians with esteem. She blesses them and praises them. But above all, she controls them. The bishop, who may be no theologian himself, can reprehend the theologian and even correct him. The theologian is under the hierarchy.

He is also useful to the hierarchy and herein lies his ecclesiastical function. The theologians are the Church's first means of developing dogma which is the official teaching of the magisterium. By their efforts the theologians recognize submerged elements in the total tradition and bring them to view. They synthesize what Scripture and tradition affirm in a way adequate for the age and place they live in. They deepen the understanding of already existing dogmas. They can be a defense for the Church in her encounter with error. It is no wonder, then, that bishops want theologians, for they can supply the hierarchs with the words and ideas which they need to communicate the revelation of Christ adequately for their time and place. The theologian is no luxury for the Church which is so vexed in her sojourn in a hostile world. He is a necessity and he himself is a Christian called by Christ to perform a Christian function.

Although many monks have been theologians and the monastery offers many facilities for theological contemplation, yet the theologian is not a monk by his own nature. We do not demand high sanctity of the theologian. Yet it is hard to see how any theologian worthy of the name can escape a stimulus to piety. If his theology thrusts him into revelation, that great meeting of God and man, something of the awe of that tremendous encounter must rub off on the theologian. There are of course theologasters, men who know the use of the theological language and the arts of theological dialectic. Such men are glib and write glibly, but they rely on the verbal structures of dogmas rather than on the revelation to which the dogma is attached. Theologasters are like mediocre lawyers, who are not interested in law and justice but only in formulae and logical verbalism. Those outside of the theological brotherhood cannot distinguish between theologian and theologaster, and they may even be more impressed by the theologaster than by the theologian. This situation is inherent in the human predicament. There is no need to rail against it. It must be accepted with resignation and equanimity.

According to this statement, then, religious understanding forms a circle. First of all there is the blinding light of revelation which is lovingly thrust on one man, called a prophet, by God in His loving condescension. This experience is not strictly verbal, though words in the imagination need not be excluded. This man has the divine commission to deliver the truth he achieved, by words to other men. His verbal communication is mediate revelation which needs in the receiver an inner enlightenment of the Holy Spirit. This prophetic communication the Church has received from the Christ and it stays with her in its verbalized and unverbalized dimension. From time to time elements of this revelation are solemnly defined and thus we have dogma. Likewise, without solemn apparatus the magisterium proposes verbal expressions whose content is undefined but authentic doctrine. Then comes the theologian who studies both dogma and doctrine and synthesizes them in terms of human intelligence which give to man a foothold in his ascent to revelation in its purity. Revelation leads to theology and theology leads to revelation. The circle is complete. The whole point is to keep the three phases of the human achievement of the divine word distinct and yet in unity. Immediate revelation is not truly verbal and it offers neither contradiction nor paradox. The mediation of this revelation by the prophet to the people involves the ambiguities of language. This again takes place in the dogmatic and doctrinal formulations of the Church's magisterium. It becomes truest when the theologian in his service to the believing Church offers his statements.

We must not suppose that every scientific discipline has its logical structure except the theological enterprise. Here the deep analogies used by the revealing God must use the logic of analogy, for this too can be delivered in valid dialectic so that intelligent consistency may be achieved. Everywhere in the transmission of God's truth analogy is used, and this does not mean figurative linguistic transfer. It always means intrinsic analogy where there is more than mere affirmation of likeness but rather the affirmation of the basic reality from which likeness flows.

VI
Church-State Relations: A Theological Consideration

In the light of recent history, it might seem to some that remarks on church-state relations could not help but have political implications. However, it must be borne constantly in mind that any remarks I make are made entirely from a theological point of view and no other. For it is only in this way that what I have to say can be read without heat by both Catholics and Protestants. Obviously, my theology is Catholic theology and constructed in that framework. There are many postulates in that system which cannot all be ventilated in a limited space. It would take too long and much of it would seem irrelevant even though the contrary is true. Above all it must be remembered that theology is a theoretical discipline. In its own order of thought abstract principles are accepted because of consistency. The application of these principles to the concrete world necessarily gives them a twist and destroys their purity. In Euclidean geometry a straight line is the shortest distance between two points; but in the world in which we live this is not necessarily true. As folk wisdom tells us, the longest way round is the shortest way home.

I am afraid that my contribution to any general discussion of the problem under review will be as tantalizing as the doctor's testimony in detective stories. In such tales the doctor is asked for the exact time of the death of the victim. His answer will always be that death could have taken place at any moment within a period of two or three hours. This information is usually not satisfactory to the police because it leaves the practical question open. The police want to know the hour and the minute of the event, but medical science cannot satisfy their curiosity. Theoretical certitudes do not easily translate themselves into practical certitudes.

It is obvious that I have surrounded myself with many precautions. It is not timidity which forces me to do so, but rather a proper prudence. The question we are discussing can be explosive and destructive. Therefore we must treat it delicately. Nothing is more distressing than to hear the question directed to Catholic theologians about the Catholic position on the relations between Church and State with the request that it be answered in a concrete context with simple affirmations or simple negations. This is impossible. A theological answer is in the abstract order in which different hypotheses must be considered. The expression of the hypotheses may sound to the lay hearer as elegant evasion or lack of candor. It is neither.

The theologian can do nothing else and still be a theologian. Two and three can be mathematically related to each other as two-thirds, one, minus one, five, or six, depending on the operation to be performed.

Now to the problem. First of all the problem is not about the relations between Church and State but rather between the sacral and the secular. For the man who denies that there is a sacral order, or affirms that it is only a phase of the secular, there is no problem. The problem consists precisely in the supposition that there are objectively two disparate orders related to each other in terms of strict otherness. Only two things can be related to each other. Where there is only one thing no relation can exist. I have no intention of proving that there is a sacral order. I assume that my readers share with me the conviction that there is such an order. Nor do I have to prove that there is a secular order because it seems too evident to need proof.

Now the sacral order is the plane, or better, the dimension of man's relationship to divinity and the secular order is the dimension of man's relationship to the world of finite realities, especially to the fellow man with whom he lives. If by the word Church we mean the sacral order and by the word State we mean the secular order, we can make certain statements which could be accepted by most men.

Let us take the case of Socrates. Obviously he was no Christian, but no one would deny that he was a noble man. He was tried by an Athenian court on the charge that he was corrupting Athenian youth by his doctrines.

The court was willing to pardon him if he promised to abstain from teaching. His answer was that he said what he had to say because of an inner voice which was divine. In consequence he could not acquiesce to the request of the court. The result was that he was executed.

All the world since the time of Socrates judges that the Greek sage was good and noble in refusing to obey his government, though all the world also thinks that disobedience to law and judicial decision is a bad thing, as Socrates himself held. This judgment of men is not paradoxical. They believe that obedience to God is in order even if this entails disobedience to the State. The Christians find this stand clearly expressed in the words of Peter when a Jewish tribunal ordered him to stop preaching the gospel. Peter said: "Whether it is right in the sight of God to listen to you rather than to God, you must judge" (Acts 4:19). Our own country respects the rights of conscientious objectors and does not demand of them that they bear arms even in time of war.

We can therefore draw the first principle on the relations between Church and State from the examples we have cited. The sacral order, distinct as it is from the order of the secular, is a superior order. Its claims are absolute and its imperatives unconditional. The secular order cannot legitimately make demands if its demands go counter to those which are sacral. We in America refer to this principle when we speak of the inviolability of conscience. This first principle is commonly accepted by mankind at large, no matter what be the individual's religion. It is also the first principle of Catholic theology.

It is an inevitable principle for anyone who declares that God is the Lord.

There is a second principle no less important than the first, though it is subordinate. The proper evolution of man supposes that he coexists and collaborates with his own kind. Aristotle put this truth in the famous phrase which says that man is a civic animal. Human society is therefore something natural and spontaneous. Complete isolation from other men is not the proper condition for human life. This hardly needs more discussion.

Now human co-existence is another way of saying that man by instinct lives in society. Society is therefore necessary for man. Sometimes no society is needed other than the family or the clan. This is the condition of nomadic peoples sparsely inhabiting large areas of land. However, sedentary people perforce co-exist with human beings of different families. Clan rules are not enough because clan is mingled with clan. Above the clan therefore there must be another pattern for living together. The highest pattern of social co-existence we call civil society and the mode of societal structure it adopts is called the state. The state is thus a source of law and only by law does it operate. It also has the means to execute those laws and the means to judge between the citizen and the law. "State" should not be considered as a synonym for civil society itself. It is rather the specific form whereby a civil society is ultimately bound together in stability in order to insure all citizens the earthly conditions necessary for each man's pursuit of happiness within the framework of human fellowship.

States are generically the same but they can be specifically different. The state is a polity and we have many kinds of polities. Some are monarchic; others are oligarchic; others still are democratic. Plato gave us this division and although it is not altogether adequate, it is good enough for our present purposes.

States are natural things because they have their origins in human nature. They are therefore nonsacral. This does not mean that the state is not under God. It, like all other creatures, is subject to the divine will. However, the state has as its purpose the worldly welfare of the community. It is not religious in its preoccupations. It looks manwards and not Godwards. It makes its laws for the human situation and must tolerate all the defects inherent in this situation. The laws of God are absolute directions for man but the state makes its laws relative to the human predicament and relative to the common good of all citizens. Divine law and human law are of quite different textures. God's law may forbid this or that action but the state may wisely permit it lest greater evil fall upon the community. The state wants to keep the community together almost at all costs because this is its only interest and concern. The state is not God and its will is not ultimate nor absolute.

Catholic theology holds as its second principle in the matter of the relations between sacral and secular that the civic community, and therefore its state, are necessary God-willed institutions. Concerning this state the Catholic Church teaches that it can take any of the forms which Plato indicated. It considers the state sovereign over its citizens so that the citizen is in conscience bound to obey the state's laws according to the tenor of these laws. So Catholics understand the Scriptural aphorism: "Render therefore to Caesar the things that are Caesar's, and to God the things that are God's" (Matt. 22:21). The concerns of the natural order must be referred to the laws of the state as guide and norm. The state is naturally competent to deal with such matters and it is autonomous, free, and authoritative in its decisions. There is no natural institution over the state, even though there is a higher human order, the sacral, which is on an altogether different level. On its own level of natural concern, the state is man's highest social institution. Nor need the state be exclusively national; it can take on international characteristics as well.

According to Catholic theology, then, man is subject to two directives and two imperatives. One is absolute and that is the sacral; the other is relative and it is the secular. But the same man at the same time is subject to both orders. From the perspective of a geometry of pure ideas God's command can never put man into conflict with the state because the state as pure idea is itself willed by God. This state, since it functions according to the dictates of nature which is divinely structured, will be no obstacle to man's obedience to sacral imperatives. In the ideal order there is a pre-established concord between the two sources of human allegiance. Hence the third Catholic principle on the relations between Church and State is that in this quite un-ideal world Church and State should strive after the closest concretely possible approximation to an ideal concord, which nevertheless never means identity.

I submit that this doctrine is reasonable and utterly conformable to the beliefs of most men. The only ones who will find difficulty with it are those who deny the sacral order or make of it a natural component of the secular order itself. Those who identify God and State, state-idolaters as we call them, or those who deny the existence of any order above the natural, will not be sympathetic to this vision. But their lack of sympathy will not be caused by the fact that the theory is Catholic but rather because it is an implicit affirmation of the lordship of a transcendental God beyond the limitations of the natural. But this implicit affirmation lies at the heart of Jewish and Protestant faiths no less than in the Catholic religion.

American non-Catholics really have no objection to the three basic principles of the Catholic theology on Church and State. They are, however, concerned with the practical understanding of the third principle which demands the greatest possible concord between the sacral and the secular. Catholics identify the sacral order with the arrangements of the organized society called the Roman Catholic Church. The principle of concord would then seem to mean from the Catholic point of view that the state must adjust all its action to the Catholic point of view. Other religions would then have no rights in the community. This, needless to say, alarms the non-Catholic deeply. He can see in the political action of the Catholic only a threat to his own freedom and existence.

It is well for Catholics to recognize this fear in non-

Catholics and understand it. The American Catholic *as a matter of fact* is not conscious of any desire to suppress all religions other than his own. He finds such an idea shocking and grotesque. He is simply bewildered when the non-Catholic accuses him of such intentions. Now most non-Catholic Americans do know that their Catholic fellow citizens have no sinister designs against them. They know that the Catholic reveres the Constitution of our country and even becomes starry-eyed when he talks about it. But the non-Catholic is afraid of what he thinks is the inner logic of the Catholic position. As long as the numerical situation does not allow the logical drives to operate, the Catholic is no menace. But, asks the non-Catholic, what will happen when the situation does not prevent logic from producing its own consequences?

I think this is the mentality of questioning non-Catholics who approach the question objectively and without antecedent bias. With these men and women the American Catholics must hold dialogue so that understanding be achieved in order to make our national unity strong. Dialogue is impossible with these non-Catholics who simply cannot tolerate the notion of a Catholic in any civic post of prominence because of the uncriticized assumption that America is a Protestant country. Catholics simply must resign themselves to the panicky shrillness of such people. Conversation is not possible with them because their minds are closed by fear and passion. No matter what you say to them, if it does not agree with their preconceived opinions about Catholics it will not be believed. And it is uncomfortable for the Catholic to be called a liar even when it is done only by implication.

But the dialogue with the open-minded non Catholic Americans is not only possible but feasible. For the last thirty years, within Catholic theology, there has been much thinking and writing on the Catholic doctrine of Church and State. Some people like to think that there is a fearful struggle going on among quarreling theologians, some coming up with something new and better and others stubbornly sticking to something old and alien. Actually this is not the situation. Theological investigation is going on and clarification is being reached by an academic debate in Catholic circles. The full investigation has not yet been ended and it will go on for some time to come.

It is wise for non-Catholics to note that one does not simply write to the Pope and ask him to answer any and every question to which he immediately gives a definitive answer. Before the Pope speaks theologians must formulate the question with accuracy. This takes time. To ask the Pope to speak before that time is fulfilled is naïve understanding. Badly constructed questions should never be answered because to such questions only badly constructed answers can be given. Such answers help no one but rather cause confusion which is one thing the Popes try to avoid at all costs. While the question evolves toward accuracy the Popes do speak but only to the presently achieved status of the question. From Leo XIII to the present Pope John XXIII we have such a series of papal pronouncements which help the theologians in their quest for the finally right form of the question.

In the debate concerning the meaning of concord between the secular and the sacral, some points of clarification are emerging. One is that the natural state operates only in terms of human law. The other is that the notion of state must be constantly revised in the light of what modern states really are. The third is that geometrical positions of abstract thought are not meant to be blueprints for concrete structures.

Certain conclusions have been recognized. The first is that human law for the human community is not a religious profession of faith nor even a prolongation of divine law. For human law to banish certain theoretically immoral things might, in a concrete case, disrupt the community because the execution of the law through wide police intrusion into private life might make life in the community intolerable. Human law is for the natural common good of all, and no laws should be made which are not necessary for that common good. Law is always restrictive on human liberty and we should not have more laws than are really needed. And as Pope Pius XII said in his address to the fifth National Convention of the Union of Italian Jurists on December 6, 1953, the national state of today must not overlook its international character in the world we live in. Religious tolerance for the late pontiff was an absolute necessity on the international level of law.

We must remember that the doctrine of the First Amendment whereby the American state has no competence to make laws concerning religious faith and practice, thus assuring fullest religious liberty in the land, is not a theological statement but a legal principle. It is a law of the land and the only question facing us is whether it is a good or bad law. From the day of the promulgation of this basic law to our time Catholics have enthusiastically accepted it as a good law, to be preserved now and in the future. In December of 1787, Archbishop John Carroll, the first Catholic bishop of our country, said in the *Columbian Magazine:* "Freedom and independence, acquired by the united efforts, and cemented with the mingled blood of Protestant and Catholic fellow citizens, should be equally enjoyed by all." A contemporary of Carroll, Bishop John England, put Carroll's thought most forcefully: "May God long preserve the liberties of America from the union of any church with state! In any country, with any religion, it is an unnatural increase of the power of the executive against the liberties of the people." From those early days to our own, bishop after bishop has made similar statements. In fact in 1948, January 25, the late Archbishop John T. McNicholas issued a statement authorized by the episcopal board of the National Catholic Welfare Council in which it is stated: "We deny absolutely and without any qualification that the Catholic bishops of the United States are seeking a union of Church and State by any endeavours whatsoever, either proximate or remote. If tomorrow Catholics constituted a majority in our country, they would not seek a union of Church and State. . . . In complete accord with the Catholic doctrine, we hold firmly that our own constitutional provisions are the best for our country. Even had we the authority to do so, we would not change one iota of them."*

As recently as 1960, on March 18, Archbishop Egidio Vagnozzi, the papal delegate to the Catholics of the United States, said magnificently at a luncheon held in his honor at Loyola University, Chicago:

> As far as the United States is concerned, I feel that it is the true interpretation of the feelings of the Hierarchy and of American Catholics in general to say that they are well satisfied with their Constitution and pleased with the fundamental freedom enjoyed by their Church; in fact, they believe that this freedom is to a large extent responsible for the expansion and consolidation of the Church in this great country. Whether they remain a minority, or become a majority, I am sure that American Catholics will not jeopardize their cherished religious freedom in exchange for a privileged position.

These are only a few pronouncements of a long and constant series of episcopal statements. I just cannot see what more assurance non-Catholic Americans can ask of Catholics. *Officially and really American Catholics do not want now or in the future a law which would make Catholicism the favored religion of this land.* They do not want the religious freedom of American non-Catholics to be curtailed in any way. They sincerely

* All the above quotations are cited from *America*, vol. 103, no. 26, Sept. 24, 1960, p. 696.

want the present First Amendment to be retained and to become ever more effective. With a note of desperation I ask, what more can we say?

The thinking Protestant is prone to accept this sincere profession of loyalty to our country. But he has qualms. He says to the Catholic: Yes, I know you think this way, but in history and even today in other lands your record is not good. How can I be sure that what has happened elsewhere will not happen here? The Catholic can only answer: Look about you! The heads of state in West Germany and France are Catholics. This is also true in Ireland. Catholics will soon be a majority in Holland. Do non-Catholics in those lands feel any oppression or do they even show any fear of such an event? If it is true that Catholicism is established by law in some countries, it is equally true that such establishment is found in lands called Protestant. In England the royal sovereign to receive the crown must swear to protect Protestantism. It may be that such laws are good laws for those communities, maybe not. The American Catholic is not concerned. He only knows that the American law of religious freedom for all citizens is excellent law for his land.

Some non-Catholic Americans feel quite assured that American Catholics do not want to and, what is more important, cannot change our American freedom of religion. They are afraid of something else. A Catholic lawmaker or a Catholic executive might deviously push Catholic moral precepts into our laws and in consequence non-Catholics would be hampered. Some shudder at the thought of a Catholic Mass being said in the White House or of the dark influence of the priest who hears the confession of a Catholic statesman.

Once more we are faced with a confusion. The function of civil law is not to teach theology or even the moral views of the legislator. In conscience, be he Catholic, Protestant, or Jew, it would be immoral for him to impose on the community what he thinks immoral. He would have to disassociate himself from such an action. However, the toleration of immorality, if such toleration is demanded by the common good, is good law, and in accord with the morality of political action. This usually is the task facing the statesman. He is not a moral philosopher nor a moral teacher. That a Catholic statesman comes to his task with a Catholic conscience is as true as the fact that a Protestant statesman comes with a Protestant conscience. But for both of these men the task is exclusively the making of good laws. The obligation of civil law is not of the same nature and scope as the obligations of the moral law. I do not say that law can prescind from morality, but I do say that the attempt to impose one moral theory or another is not the function of the statesman. Here he takes his lead from the consensus of the community. In America any elected official is a citizen designated by the people for some temporary function of state. This man has a double life. He has his own and that of a civil servant. If in his own life he wishes to worship in one way or in none, this is no political concern of the civic community. By our laws he is free in the matter. In his public role he is a man of the law which is framed for practical purposes and canonizes no philosophy or theology. I can conceive of a highly moral man who in his interior conscience considers traffic in liquor to be immoral and yet could refuse to make a law about it, or even vote for the removal of such existing legislation. He is being highly moral in his political action if he judges that such a law would do more public harm than good.

As for the guidance which a Catholic man of state receives from a competent confessor, I need only state that any priest would insist that the prime obligation of the statesman is to enact laws for the common good of his concrete community according to its unique history and character, or to execute such laws already made. The confessor's service to his client is exclusively private, moral, and religious. He has no competence in political matters which belong not to the order of morality and piety but to the order of law. Nor do I think that a Catholic president will have Mass in the White House. He knows that this would be displeasing to many of the people in whose name and power he acts. It could far more easily happen in the term of a non-Catholic president because he would not be suspected of pushing Catholicism. It has been my experience that Catholics are less embarrassed when dealing with non-Catholic political figures than with one of their own. With the Catholic office holder we are over-careful to do nothing which would cause comment. As for the interference of the bishops or the Pope, it can be said without hesitation that there will be none of it. The Pope does not meddle with the political activity of Adenauer or de Gaulle, nor would either man permit it. The Catholic president's comportment with the clergy of his church will be exactly like the comportment of a Protestant president with the clergy of his church. Both will give the clergy the same social deference which the community at large grants them—no more and no less.

To all non-Catholics I would suggest that they keep in mind the difference of the order of law which is the political concern and the order of religion and ethics which is the believer's concern. The two are not the same nor do they produce conflicts *per se*. The morality of divorce, birth-control, liquor traffic, and the like are one thing. Civil legislation about them is quite another. Morality is categorical and obliges by inner consent. Legislation is conditioned and works by some kind of external coercion. Let non-Catholics also remember that the theological questions involved in the relations of the Church today with the modern State are still in the process of exact formation. You cannot hurry such a process and it is rather annoying and irrelevant to ask questions which are hardly as simple as the questioner believes. Nor should we consider a pure geometry of Church-State relationships as a practical guide for action in the concrete world. Above all, non-geometers should not geometrize for us. We shall do better by ourselves.

I conclude with a personal testimony. I have been working in theology for over thirty years. I have always admired and loved my country with its institutions and history. I can sincerely say that there is absolutely nothing in Catholic theology which prevents a Catholic from holding public office on any level according to the spirit and letter of our American law.

VII
The Eastern Churches and Reunion

Because the ecumenical movement is a palpable force at work in the Christian Churches, we see on all sides stirrings toward church mergers. In 1938, the largest of the Methodist churches in the United States united to become The Methodist Church. Canada has its United Church embracing Presbyterians, Methodists, and Congregationalists. The Congregationalists of the United States have joined with the Evangelical and Reformed Church to produce the United Church of Christ. The Church of South India is a lively church fusing Anglicans, Presbyterians, and others. A Church of North India is in the making now, following the pattern of the South India Church. Different Lutheran churches in America are contemplating a vast merger which will be called the American Lutheran Church.

More such unions within Protestantism could be mentioned. On the Catholic side there is a strong movement to bring the 500,000 Malinkarese Jacobites of Malabar into union with Rome. There is every hope that this will take place very soon. The Catholic Chaldeans are steadily absorbing the Assyrian Nestorians who are only a small remnant in Mesopotamia. However, although there are Catholic non-Latin churches among the Copts and Ethiopians, there are no signs of any large scale reunion interest on the part of the Ethiopians and the Copts.

The great oriental church is, of course, the Eastern Orthodox sisterhood of churches. Because the vast majority of them are under the political jurisdiction, direct or indirect, of Russia, it is hard to be exact in giving their numbers. But it is not unreasonable to say that an objective census would discover a figure between 100 and 200 millions of them all over the world. Certainly the Greek churches are interested in the current reunion movements. The Ecumenical Patriarch's jurisdiction, the Great Church of Constantinople, belongs to the World Council of Churches. So does the Church of Greece. None of the Orthodox churches behind the Iron Curtain has joined but the Patriarchate of Moscow has made application for admission into the World Council. Political pressures may well explain such activity. Toward the Catholic Church and its present Pope, John XXIII, the Ecumenical Patriarch of Constantinople, Athenagoras, has shown courtesy and friendliness.

This attitude of the Patriarch has been shared by other Orthodox churches. The Russian Orthodox outside of Russia are quite willing to enter into dialogue with

Catholics, be it in or out of a World Council context. The Metropolitan of the Syrian Orthodox Church in America seems to have the same sentiments.

Actually, in Europe and America there are informal Orthodox-Catholic conversations. Nothing very spectacular has come forth but anyone engaged in such meetings knows how amicable they are and how fruitful they have been for mutual understanding and appreciation.

But what has been achieved is not yet highly significant. What are the chances of Orthodox-Catholic reunion? It is impossible to give a certain answer to this question. It can safely be said that they are better than they were one hundred years ago. With equal safety it can be said that the chances for immediate reunion are too slim to found any hope for any program of wide efficacy.

Yet the reunion of the Orthodox and Catholic Churches is more in the order of probability than the union of Protestants and Catholics. There is so much that the Orthodox and Catholics share that they can meet without raising questions which would necessarily vex a Catholic-Protestant dialogue. The atmosphere of Orthodox-Catholic conversation is easy. Both sides have quite similar if not identical attitudes to the Church. In both churches tradition is understood and used. The liturgies of the two communions are substantially the same. No one has to defend the principle of the hierarchic structure of the Church; it is spontaneously taken for granted. Mariology, and icon-veneration are antecedently accepted by both. The normative value of the first Seven Councils is sincerely accepted by both groups. That

Eastern Orthodoxy and Roman Catholicism were one for at least a thousand years is well remembered.

A superficial observer might wonder what keeps these two churches apart. But when we go deeper than superficiality, we note that there are serious obstacles to union. The historic evolutions of the two churches have been very different. The stances of piety and theological method are distinct. The resentments produced centuries ago because of the mistakes on both sides have frozen hard the alienation of the two communities. The efficacious desire for union has not been too strong on either side.

Yet in spite of all these highly significant things, union is not out of the question. When dealing with Protestants the Catholic Church in logic must demand of them conversion. This is hard for a man who is devotedly attached to his church. Perhaps on ultimate reduction this too must be demanded of the Orthodox but it will not have the appearance of so radical a change. Catholics do not rebaptize Orthodox who enter into Roman communion; they do not reordain; they do not demand that the Orthodox change their liturgical practice and local church customs. The Orthodox act in the same way with reference to Catholics entering into their union. They may not do it on principle, but they certainly do it by economy. The average Orthodox believer who does not know theology but leads his religious life by use of the liturgy in communion with his hierarchy would notice absolutely no change if Orthodoxy and Catholicism became one. He would still call himself an orthodox Christian.

But the *o* would be small, just as in the Latin mass the congregation prays for all "orthodox worshippers of the Catholic and apostolic faith." Likewise every Orthodox by his own designation belongs to the "orthodox, Catholic and apostolic Church of the East." Orthodoxy and Catholicism are dear both to Orthodox and Catholic believers.

Even in the prickly field of theology, matters are formidable but not impossible. In the light of the Seven Councils and the holy liturgies, the Orthodox can now see what Catholic formulas are after. Catholic theologians can, in terms of their own doctrine, give acceptable meaning to Orthodox formulae. Today neither Church is intransigeant to the other and there is a readiness to analyze disputed questions with as much serenity as the long separation permits. The Orthodox do believe that the Romans are heretical as a Church, but the Catholics do not consider the Orientals as an heretical church but only a church in schism, even though individual theologians may well hold heretical positions.

The great hurdle to be passed is the question of the significance and function of the Pope of Rome. The Catholic position is now definitive because of the decrees of the Vatican Council. But the Vatican doctrine is obnoxious and impious from the viewpoint of all Orthodox theologians. However, even here the impasse is neither rigid nor total. Whatever the Orthodox think of the position of the Pope after 1054, they yet admit that until that time the bishop of Rome was the first patriarch of the Church. They willingly admit papal primacy but do not give that term any juridical or definitive power. For them the Patriarch of Constantinople is now the first patriarch but they concede that in the event of reunion the Pope would again be the primatial hierarch. Just what his powers would be can be the subject of exploratory investigation. Not a few Orthodox would be willing to give the Pope powers that their predecessors would not have granted. Today they rather defend regional autonomies which, however, are not absolute. Much can be done with this stand and Catholic theologians could find formulas which would neither compromise the Vatican decrees nor yet deny principles involved in the theories of the Orthodox. In this field much work must still be done by the theologians of both Churches for they have barely begun the work.

The possibilities of reunion are, therefore, real. But sheer possibility does not imply probability. The purpose of this exposé is not to raise hopes of a union which is really desired by both Churches, but without passion. The real difficulties militating against the union derive from existential factors rather than from theological differences. There is engrained both in Catholics and Orthodox the unanalyzed feeling that the other party is treacherous, blind to the truth, and sinfully bull-headed. When this attitude to the partner in dialogue is deep and strong, not too much can be done. Individuals on either side may well be free of such prejudices but they know very well that their own correligionaries are obsessed by them. Each side is demanding from the other total surrender which, of course, neither side is willing to accept.

During the last fifty years this problem has been seen by intelligent men in both camps. They have spoken and their words have not been without fruit, but when so many millions are involved the work is slow.

What makes this situation lasting is the fact that the two communities are geographically and spiritually isolated one from each other. The little missionary work done by Catholics in Orthodox territory makes a few individual converts but only irritates the Orthodox community as a whole. In the West the Orthodox do not engage in any organized missionary activity. Each collectivity works without any dependence on the other and each has ample territory to work in.

In the past two brief reunion periods feebly existed. The second Council of Lyons (1274) and the Council of Florence (1438–45) produced paper unions with no lasting effects. On both occasions the Greek Orthodox were in a precarious political position. They were facing the threat of an invasion and domination by Islam. The two Eastern emperors wanted the aid of the West and felt that religious union would supply them with military assistance. The union was not desired by the people of the East and the West felt no need to help the Byzantines. By the thirteenth century, with all the evils produced in the time of the Crusades, the Orthodox frankly stated that they preferred the turban of Mahomet to the tiara of the Pope.

Yet political conditions can influence the emotional impasse afflicting the Churches. Current Russian Orthodoxy in its days of travail could not appeal for help beyond Russia and ultimately had to make peace with the Soviet government which, though hostile, found itself impotent to destroy the Church, and in consequence was ready for a concordat which was to its own advantage. But the condition of Greek Orthodoxy is different. It is fairly independent in Muslim lands and in Europe enjoys the favor of the Greek government. But it nevertheless stands between two mighty foes. From the south there looms the strong Pan-Arabic movement which is intensely Muslim. To the north stands the antireligious Communist colossus with imperialistic designs on the Levant. This precarious position makes Byzantium look westward with a gaze less than angry. Yet it would be foolish to make any prophecies in the light of this vague situation. But it is also true that if both bodies felt that their own existences were in serious danger, they might well be attracted to each other for consolation and support.

Then there was the action of Pope John XXIII who spent years in regions of Orthodoxy and is well-favored toward its people. When he announced on January 25, 1959, that he would convoke a general council, he also insinuated that this might be the occasion of union with non-Catholic Christians, and he made it clear that he was thinking of the Orthodox most of all. The Ecumenical Patriarch of Constantinople received the news with graciousness, but announced that he would do nothing outside of the World Council framework.

So in the Autumn of 1960 Cardinal Domenico Tardini, head of the antepreparatory commission for the future

Council, announced that non-Catholics would have no seat or voice in the Council but they would be welcome to ask for permission to attend the Council as observers. This invitation would not be directed to particular groups but addressed to the non-Catholic world in general.

Under these circumstances it is hard to say what the Orthodox churches will do with reference to the second Vatican Council. They may well ignore it altogether and merely await to see the results therein achieved. It is hard to be optimistic in the face of this reserve on both sides.

What is needed is a willingness on the part of both churches to come together in meetings outside of an ecumenical council where the objective will be not reunion but mutual understanding and friendliness. If these two values can be achieved, then the moment will be ripe to discuss the further question which is the question of reunion. It is impossible at the moment to make any predictions concerning the probability of the first but indispensable step. To all who believe in the desire of Christ that we all be one and who according to Christ's command love their neighbor, one needful action is imperative. We must pray to God for union. Such prayer brings the warmth of heaven to melt the frosts of centuries. It also prepares the hearts of those who pray for a fraternal approach to an alienated brother. This much we can all do. What is more, it is something that with urgency we must do.